SEF

The Rise and Fall

Cover illustration: Emperor Stephen Dushan (1331-55)

For Milovje Vasic
who first aroused my interest in Yugoslavia

SERBIA

The Rise and Fall
of a
Medieval Empire

by
Thomas Durham, B.A., Hist. (London)

William Sessions Limited,
York, England

Copyright Thomas Durham

© 1989

Thomas Durham is a history graduate of London University and taught history in Edinburgh from 1957-1980.

ISBN 1 85072 060 6

Printed in 10/11 point Plantin
by William Sessions Limited
The Ebor Press, York, England

Contents

Chapter		Page
	Preface	vii
I	The Making of the State	1
II	The Serbian Empire	31
III	Dushan and Constantinople	47
	Relations with Venice and New Wars with Byzantium	47
	Relations with Bulgaria	66
	Relations with Hungary and the Papacy	72
IV	Urosh and the Fall of the Empire	81
V	The Serbians in Voivodina	100
VI	Church, State and Economy	114
	Bibliography	135
	Index	137

I am indebted to Dumbarton Oaks Publications for permission to use the map from Soulis (G.C.) *Serbs and Byzantium*.

Preface

I FIRST BECAME INTERESTED IN Yugoslavia as a result of meeting a Serbian exile in Paris in 1947, who had the misfortune to fight on the 'wrong' side during the Second World War. My original intention had been to write a book on the formation of the Yugoslav state after 1918. I soon found, however, that a number of questions arose in the course of my research, which could only be satisfactorily answered, if at all, by studying the early history of the various provinces which make up the state of Yugoslavia, and it seemed to me that the key to the problems which had prevented the creation of a unified South Slav state, as well as the problems which faced Yugoslavia after unification had been achieved, lay in the past.

There seemed to be no books in English covering the history of medieval Serbia. The standard works on the Byzantine Empire make frequent references to the Slavs, both as subjects and enemies of the Empire, particularly the Bulgarians, and these works have provided valuable information for the book I decided to write. But a number of questions remained unanswered. It is easy to see why the South Slavs should have been influenced, in law, politics and religion by Byzantium. But why should the Croats, for instance, have adopted the Catholic rather than the Orthodox faith, and the Latin rather than the Cyrillic alphabet? This is not merely a matter of historical interest; the tragic consequences of this religious difference became very clear during the war when the Croat puppet government massacred thousands of Serbians.

This is not a work of original scholarship; many of the sources from which the early history of Serbia can be studied are to be found in the Chronicles and Histories of the Greek historians, particularly Cantacuzene and Gregoras, but as I know no Greek, I was unable to benefit from them. Where there are Serbian sources I have used them, in particular Danilo's lives of the Serbian kings and archbishops, and the Greek Charters of the Serbian kings which are provided with a Serbian translation. For the most part I have relied on secondary works in Serbo-Croat, Russian and German. If this book encourages younger students with more time than I have had to undertake further research in this field, it will have served its purpose.

Serbian Rulers

Stephen Nemanja Great Zupan	1166- 1196
Stephen First Crowned (king from 1217)	1196-c1223
Stephen Radoslav	c1223-c1234
Stephen Urosh	1243- 1276
Stephen Dragutin	1276- 1282
Stephen Urosh Milutin	1282- 1321
Stephen Urosh Dechanski	1321- 1331
Stephen Dushan (emperor from 1345)	1331- 1355
Stephen Urosh	1355- 1371
(King Vukashin)	1366- 1371
Prince Lazar	1371- 1389
Stephen Lazarevich (from 1402 Despot)	1389- 1427
George Brankovich (from 1429 Despot)	1427- 1456
Lazar Brankovich	1456- 1458

CHAPTER I

The Making of the State

SERBIAN POWER WAS ESTABLISHED relatively late in the Balkans; the inability or unwillingness of the Slav tribes to submit to the domination of one ruler made it impossible for them to assert their independence from the emperors at Constantinople. The first successful attempt to establish independence from Byzantium was made by the Bulgarians under Tsar Simeon and later Samuel who created the first Bulgarian Empire and threatened the existence of the Byzantine Empire. The great victory of Basil II over Samuel removed the menace of Bulgaria for more than a century. During the long struggle between Bulgaria and Byzantium the Serbians were the victims of one or other of these two powers.

Two branches of the South Slavs, the Serbians and the Croats, inhabited the western part of the Balkan peninsula, but from the outset they differed in their political and ultimately their religious development. By the ninth century the Croats had become increasingly subject to Western influence – Frankish and Venetian – had adopted the Catholic religion and the Latin alphabet, and abandoned the Zupan form of political organisation which predominated among the other South Slavs in favour of monarchy, and eventually accepted the King of Hungary as their ruler. Henceforth Croats and Serbians pursued different policies but it is important to remember that they were one people.

In Serbia proper the tribal system of government – if one can call it so, existed prior to their settlement in the Balkans. This system was based on the Zupa, under the leadership of the Zupan who maintained an independent role, though subordinate to the over-lordship of the Emperor in Constantinople. In time the Zupans came to recognise the nominal rule of the Great Zupan, one that is who had achieved enough power and influence to make his position effective. The emergence of such a figure and the willingness of the other Zupans to submit to his authority created a situation favourable for the creation of a Serbian state. Circumstances favouring the development of such a state did not arise until about the end of the 12th century. Even at its greatest extent, however, in the reign of Stephen Dushan, the Serbian state at no time contained all the South Slavs; this failure to create a large compact South Slav state was due in part to geographical factors.

From the 10th century we can distinguish seven territories inhabited by Serbians. In the southern coastal areas of the Balkans, Zeta stretched from the mouth of the Drina to the coast at Kotor, including part of modern Montenegro and separated from Ras or Rascie by the River Zeta. Trebinje or Travinja was contiguous with Zeta near Rudnik and Kotor and extended to Dubrovnik. Hum or Zahumlje (the modern Hercegovina) extended from Dubrovnik to the mouth of the Neretsa. In the 10th century Pagania or Neretania included the coast between the Neretsia and Tsetinje, and in the north extended to the Danube, including the islands of Korcula, Mlet, Hvar and Brac. To the north lay Serbia proper, or Ras and Bosnia. The boundary between Ras and Bosnia followed the course of the Rivers Drina and part of the Lim. Bosnia extended as far north as the Sava. The territories of Ras extended between the Drina and the Bulgarian Morava and took in the basin of the Serbian Morava and Ibar, while in the north the border extended almost as far as the Danube. Another Serbian area was Podgora. Thus the various Serbian territories were separated geographically and the links between them were weak. While, as we have seen, one Zupan emerged who was able to establish his authority over the others, this authority up to the 12th century was nominal. Nor was the office of Great Zupan the prerogative of one family or one territory. In the majority of cases the office was held by the Zupan of Ras or Zeta but could go elsewhere. The result was that the political centre of Serbia was constantly changing.

Other external factors hindered the development of a strong state. First the acknowledgment of Byzantine supremacy which had been accepted from the earliest period of settlement, itself the consequence rather than the cause of disunity. Under a weak emperor this supremacy might be nominal, but it was not seriously challenged until the advent of the Great Zupan, Stephen Nemanje, and then only because of the difficulties facing the Empire as a result of the Crusades and the Bulgarian rising which culminated in the formation of the Second Bulgarian Empire. The resurgence of Bulgarian power, however welcome in weakening the power of Byzantium, at the same time posed a threat to the Serbians. In extending their power at the expense of the Slav provinces of the Empire, the Bulgarians were advancing towards territories which could be considered rightly Serbian. The fact that the Serbians were divided and that the Zupans were concerned primarily with the protection of their own lands, and were ready to submit to Bulgarian domination, made the task of the latter easier.

The Bulgarian rising against Byzantium, led by the brothers Peter and Asen, probably of Vlach origin, which led to the formation of the Second Bulgarian Empire, was a more serious threat to the existence of the Byzantine Empire than had been the case with the first Empire of Simeon. On that occasion the absence of any other threat had made it possible for the Emperor to deploy the formidable military and economic power it still possessed against the Bulgarians and this had led to the complete destruction of Bulgaria as an independent state. By the end of the 12th century the situation had changed with the rise of Hungary and the threat from the West from the Crusaders under the leadership of Frederick Barbarossa, a threat exacerbated by the religious question. At that period the Serbians were probably the least dangerous threat to the Empire, but the situation offered advantages if the Serbians could form alliances with one or other of the enemies of Byzantium.

It was Ras which provided the nucleus around which the state of Serbia would grow. With the emergence of the Zupan of Ras, Stephen Nemanje, a new period in the history of the Serbian people began, and it was from Ras that resistance to Byzantium began. Strategically well placed owing to its geographical position, it was able to attract within its orbit nearly all the Serbian lands and form a powerful state. But more than 50 years were to pass before Ras became the political centre of the Serbian people. The domination of Ras had already begun before the emergence of Nemanje, but within the territories now being absorbed the tribal system continued to exist, a situation which remained unchanged throughout the whole of the subsequent history of Serbia, and which in the end was to prove fatal to its political stability and very existence. At the same time not all the Serbian lands had been freed from Byzantine rule; these included southern Ras and the lands south of the Danube. The coastal areas of the west had already lost their independence; the greater part of Pagania and the islands belonging to it were controlled by Croatia – which meant in practice Hungary – while after 1120 Bosnia became an appendage of the Hungarian crown.

Serbia and her neighbours

In the year 1185 a revolution in Constantinople dethroned Andronicus I and elevated Isaac Angelos to the throne. The situation was serious; a Norman army had captured Thessalonica and was advancing towards the capital. The defeat of the Norman army led to a peace treaty between Isaac and William II of Sicily which removed the immediate danger to the Empire as far as its European possessions were concerned. The next threat came from Bulgaria. In 1186 two brothers, Peter and Kalopeter or Asen raised a revolt against Byzantine rule. The war against the Normans and the internal weakness of the Empire after the overthrow of Andronicus limited the ability of the Emperor to crush the revolt. The new Bulgarian state was recognised by the Emperor, Peter assumed the title of tsar, and the new kingdom with its capital at Trnovo, is generally known as the Second Bulgarian Empire.

When in 1183 war broke out between Hungary and Byzantium, Nemanje formed an alliance with the Hungarians as a result of which the Serbian ruler obtained the town of Nish, perhaps as a reward for his support. When, however, Isaac concluded a family alliance with the Hungarian King, which was directed against the enemies of the Empire among whom the Serbians must obviously be included, Nemanje countered by entering into alliance with Bulgaria. The alliance between Serbia and Bulgaria must have been concluded in the early years of the Bulgarian revolt although the expansion of the Serbians towards Byzantium undoubtedly followed after 1187. At the same time Nemanje was occupied with the not less important area on the western frontier of Serbia, namely Dalmatia. Here the situation was complicated by the fact that Frederick Barbarossa claimed the Norman rights to Dalmatia as a result of the marriage of his son Henry with Constance which effectively meant the union of Germany and Sicily.

In 1187 news was reached in the East that a great Crusading army was massing under the leadership of Barbarossa in Germany who 40 years earlier had taken part in the second Crusade. This was particularly alarming in view of the hostile relations existing between the German Emperor and Manuel. For the rulers of Serbia and Bulgaria, however, the arrival of the Crusaders created a situation from which they could derive definite advantages. In 1188 ambassadors from Nemanje 'legati Serviagensis regis' arrived in Nuremburg bearing letters in which Nemanje expressed great joy, 'summa gaudio' at the prospect of the Crusading armies marching through his territories, and expressed the hope of a meeting with the Emperor. Serbian aims, however, conflicted with those of Frederick who claimed this territory on behalf of Sicily. Nemanje attempted to satisfy his claims without alienating Frederick by proposing a marriage between his son and the daughter of the Duke of Dalmatia as a means of uniting Dalmatia and Serbia. The difficulty for Frederick was to satisfy Nemanje without at the same time offending Sicily and Hungary. At a time when the relations between the Crusading leaders threatened to erupt into war, the offer of Serbian help could not be lightly disregarded. Nemanje promised to do homage to Frederick for his lands 'altera autem die venit dux (of Serbia) et facit domino imperator homonium ab ipso terram suam jure beneficario'.

Rapprochement between the Crusaders and the Slavs was not in the interests of Hungary, however, and the Hungarian King Bela withdrew his support from the Crusaders. The emergence of a strong Slav state in the

Balkans was not in the interests of Hungary, and since this was also the policy of Byzantium, the two powers were united on that issue.

Frederick would no doubt have come to an agreement with Nemanje had it been possible to satisfy the latter over Dalmatia, but in spite of his failure to obtain possession of these lands Nemanje could only benefit from the hostility between Byzantium and the Crusaders. His offer to submit as vassal to Frederick for the lands he held, provided he were allowed to retain the territories he had conquered from Byzantium, would provide him with support in the event of the Byzantine Emperor attempting to recover them, while submission to an overlord who in the normal course of events was far away, would not be onerous.

In 1190 Frederick seems to have thought seriously of accepting the military help offered by Peter of Bulgaria, but he hesitated over recognising the independence of Bulgaria and Peter's imperial title. Frederick's main aim in being in the Balkans was to obtain a peaceful passage through Byzantine territory to the Holy Land, so that, while considering the proposals of Nemanje he was also negotiating with the Emperor Isaac. Nemanje, concluding that Frederick had nothing to offer, attacked Byzantium on his own account. Under pressure from Bela III of Hungary, Isaac signed an agreement granting free passage to the Crusaders through Asia Minor. The agreement concluded between the two emperors was a blow to the Serbians and Bulgarians who now used the troops rejected by Frederick for an attack on Byzantium.

The departure of the Crusaders plus the alliance with Hungary enabled Isaac to deploy all his forces against the Slavs. Isaac determined to deal first with Bulgaria. But the Empire, threatened by risings in Asia Minor, was in no position to wage a major war against Bulgaria and failed to inflict a defeat on the old enemy. Nemanje, allied with the Bulgarians, was able to take advantage of the Emperor's difficulty to extend his territories at the expense of the Empire; he seized and destroyed Prizren and Skopje and a series of Byzantine towns in the vicinity of Strum. In 1190, however, he suffered a defeat at the hands of the Emperor and was forced to make peace. The defeat cannot have been as drastic as for instance Nicetas makes out, in view of the comparatively lenient terms which followed the victory, and the Serbian leader retained a significant part of the Byzantine territories he had conquered: in the east the area between the Rudnik valley and the central Morava with the valley of the Lepnits, Belits and Leviac; in the south of the whole area of Kosovo Field with the banks of the Rivers Sitnits and Laba. Some gains were made in Albania. The final acquisition was the littoral of Dioclea or Zeta with the towns of Skadar, Bar and Kotor. It only remained for Serbia to acquire the towns of Antivar, Scutari and Cattaro to unite all the Serbian lands under one sovereign. This is true, however, only if one regards the Bosnians and Croats as distinct peoples. (Florinskii, the Russian historian of the South Slavs, criticises the Serbian rulers for failing to unite all the 'Serbian' peoples into one state, and for wasting their energies against the Byzantine Empire.)

In the world of the Middle Ages formal recognition of a ruler was as important, perhaps more important, than the acquisition of territory by conquest in that it legitimised such acquisitions. The very fact that Isaac treated with Nemanje was an indication of the recognition of Serbian independence. Peace was strengthened by the marriage between Nemanje's son Stephen, who received the title of Sebastocrat, and Eudokia the niece of the Emperor. Marriage with a Byzantine princess and the granting of an important Byzantine title were great honours for a barbarian, bringing the Serbian ruler within the Byzantine hierarchy.

All attempts to defeat the Bulgarians proved fruitless and Isaac turned for help to his son-in-law Bela III, renewing a link with the King of Hungary which had been weakened as a result of the Hungarian attack on Serbia. Relying on Hungarian support, Isaac mounted a new offensive against Bulgaria, but in April 1195 he was overthrown by his brother Alexis and blinded. The change of Emperor had important consequences for Byzantium's relations with Serbia. The fact that the father-in-law of Stephen Nemanje was now Emperor was a factor in the change of ruler in Serbia when in 1196 Nemanje announced his intention to abdicate in favour of his son. It might have been expected that Stephen's rule would inaugurate a new era in the relations between Serbia and the Empire, but Byzantium was too weak to take advantage of the favourable situation.

The strongest influence in Ras and Bosnia was exercised by the Roman Catholic Church. With the capture of the lands of the Adriatic littoral, Nemanje had come into contact with the Archbishop of Dubrovnik and Bar. When he was conducting negotiations with Frederick, Nemanje received a letter from the Pope to his 'dear son' in which he recommended the Archbishop Bernard of Dubrovnik, whose diocese spread over Serbian lands. In the same way Stephen accepted in a friendly spirit a letter from the Pope, assured the latter of his loyalty and citing the example of his father 'nos autem semper consideramus in vestigia sancte Romane ecclesie sicut bone memorie pater meus' and recalling the numerous gifts made by his father not only to the churches in the East but also to those in the West, such as the Church of Peter and Paul in Rome and St. Nicholas in Bari. In eastern Serbia, however, the Orthodox Church maintained its supremacy. Even before becoming Great Zupan, Nemanje had begun to build monasteries, the most famous being that of Studenica. The younger son of Nemanje, Rastislav, had already entered the monastery of Vatoped, a decision on his part which was to have important consequences for the future position of the Church in Serbia, forging a link between Church and State stronger possibly than anywhere else in Europe. Constantinople was the capital of the Orthodox Church, but the Church extended beyond the borders of the Empire to Bulgaria and as far away as Novgorod. Though in matters of doctrine the Church in Serbia remained Orthodox, it was still conceived on national lines. The flirtation with Rome which took place from time to time was usually part of diplomatic manoeuvres.

In making his renunciation of the throne Nemanje regulated the succession, naming his eldest son Stephen as Great Zupan and granting to his younger son Vuk who, even in the lifetime of his father had borne the title of Great Prince, the lands of Duclea (Zeta) and Trebinje, Hvos near Pec and Toplits. Significantly these lands were widely scattered; the creation of a powerful counter state could be avoided. He also bore the old kingly title of Duclea, which he may have acquired through marriage with some princess of the old ruling house. Nemanje himself became a monk, adopting the name of Simeon and withdrew to the monastery of Studenica. Rastilic (who had adopted the name of Sava) and Stephen determined to build a monastery on Mount Athos to commemorate the dynasty and for the benefit of Serbian monks – the monastery of Hilander.

The expansion of the State

The future of the Serbian state, as for the whole of south-east Europe, was determined by the Latin conquest of Constantinople in 1204. The old Greek Empire fell, never to be completely restored; by the time the capital had been restored in 1261 the Serbian state had extended its frontiers far to the south. The kings of Hungary, former allies of Serbia, now attempted to bring the lands of Serbia under their control, leading to constant fighting between the two states. The main Slav rival, Bosnia, was expanding from the valley of the Neretsa to the Adriatic coast. Common hostility to the Angevin rulers of Hungary brought Serbia and Venice into alliance. In the complex political situation in the Balkan peninsula in the 13th century Greeks and Serbians, Franks and Hungarians fought for a supremacy none could achieve, while Albania and Montenegro frequently changed hands.

Nemanje was succeeded by his son Stephen 'certainly the most gifted of the Nemanje dynasty' who continued the work of his father. In a critical period he maintained his position against his external enemies and his rivals within the State, and took advantage of every favourable opportunity to assert the political and religious independence of Serbia. Fighting broke out again between Serbia and Hungary when Andrew, the younger brother of Bela, having assumed the title Duke of Dalmatia and Croatia, added to these that of Duke of Hum. Advancing to Zadar he boasted of his victory over Ras and Hum. Meanwhile the unsuccessful war between Bulgaria and

Byzantium was brought to an end, and was followed by the murder of Asen and Peter in Bulgaria and the succession of the third brother John Kalojan as Tsar.

In the year 1201 the young Alexis, son of Isaac, left Constantinople to seek help from the West to liberate his father and restore him to the throne. The following year a small Crusading army was assembled at Venice, under the command of Count Boniface Montferrat. Whatever the motives may have been for the Crusade, and whether as is sometimes alleged, the Venetians deliberately tried to divert the Crusaders from the Holy Land and against Constantinople, they certainly hoped to gain advantage from the men and money they were prepared to supply. Alexis could see the opportunity which the Crusaders offered to himself and tried to win the support of the Pope but met with a cool response. In view of the inability of the Crusaders to pay the Venetians, the latter refused to allow them to leave until the accounts had been settled. The Doge suggested that payment might be postponed and proposed that in view of the rebellion in Zadar the troops might be used to crush it. Failing to win support of the Pope, Alexis then turned to the German Emperor who, however, informed him that he lacked the means to help him, and advised him to turn to Venice where the Franks were preparing an expedition to Syria; a promise to work for the union of the Churches would strengthen his position. The decision of the Crusaders to advance on Constantinople was condemned by the Pope; the claim made in the Chronicle of Morea that Innocent encouraged the Franks 'dandogli indulgenzia pleniaria a tutti quelli che andavano' is clearly incorrect. In fact he threatened them with excommunication, partly because the Crusade had been planned in the first place against the Moslems, and partly because an attack on Constantinople would seriously damage the prospect of Church unity.

On the first attack against the city Alexis fled, the Crusaders liberated Isaac, and 'filio Alexi coronam imposuerunt'. For this great benefit Alexis promised to maintain for one year the army of the Crusaders. His failure to keep his word need not necessarily have been due to bad faith; indeed it was in his own interests to see the Crusaders safely away from the capital. It is more likely that money could not be found. He also promised that if the Crusaders wished to spend the winter with him in the capital, he himself would go on pilgrimage with them. Thus in the words of the Chronicle 'ita facta concordia inter Graecos et Latinos'; if so it did not last long. An insurrection broke out in the capital, the son-in-law of Alexis III was proclaimed Emperor, Isaac and the young Alexis were deposed and killed. The overthrow and death of Alexis removed any inhibitions the Crusaders might have had about attacking Constantinople and the city fell in 1204. This was an event of the very greatest importance for the peoples of the

Balkans. Although Serbians and Bulgarians had fought and won their independence from the Empire, they could hardly envisage a world in which the Empire and the centre of the Orthodox Church did not exist. Echoes of the fall were heard as far away as Novgorod.

Baldwin of Flanders was elected Emperor in place of Boniface of Montferrat and he was crowned in St. Sophia. In compensation Boniface was to receive Asia Minor and Peleponnese, together with Crete, but a quarrel broke out between him and the Emperor over the division of the spoils. Hoping to obtain the support of Venice, Boniface ceded to the Venetians his claim to Crete, and finally finished up with Thessalonika in western Thrace between the Maritsa and Vardar. So far as the Emperor's possessions were concerned, three eighths of Constantinople were to go to the Venetians including St. Sophia. All lands lying to the west of the Emperor's territories were to fall to Venice and the lands of the western Peleponnese (the Morea) as well as Epirus. The Doge was 'lord of a fourth and a half of the whole empire of Romania'. The Venetians occupied St. Sophia with the words 'the Empire is yours we will have the Patriarchate' (imperium est vestrum nos habebi mus patriarcham). One cannot therefore speak of the Latin Empire; the power of the Emperor was severely limited. In any case Baldwin was not destined to enjoy his power for long; in 1205 he was defeated by the Bulgarians and probably killed. He was succeeded by his brother Henry.

The fall of the Greek Empire created an entirely new situation in the Balkans and effectively ended the alliance of Stephen with Byzantium. Even before the fall of the capital, Stephen had dismissed his wife Eudokia, daughter of Alexis III, and attempted to establish closer relations with the West with the object of gaining a crown from the Pope. On the occasion of a Council at Bar in the territory of his brother Vukan he promised the Pope as 'patri suo' that he would send an ambassador with a request that the Pope should send a legate with a crown. Such an opportunity for extending the power and influence of the Catholic Church was not to be missed. This move, however, was strongly opposed by the King of Hungary who, in a letter to the Pope clearly showed that he wished to prevent the development of friendly relations between the Papacy and Serbia. Opposition also came from Vukan who, bearing the title of King in his own lands, no doubt believed one king to be enough in the Serbian lands. Stephen did not obtain his crown until 1217.

Relations between Stephen and Vukan deteriorated rapidly after the death of Nemanje, due in part to the fact that the former as eldest brother had been passed over in favour of Stephen. The struggle for power which followed between the two brothers was not confined to Serbia; Hungary and Bulgaria were both involved. The Bulgarian Tsar Kalojan, taking advantage of the Latin attack on Constantinople, occupied the western territories of the Empire, taking the cities of Prizren, Skopje, Ohrid and Bera. Resistance came from the King of Hungary, Imre, and in the course of the fighting he seized some episcopates which the tsar regarded as rightly Bulgarian. Serbia was drawn into the war with which the civil strife became linked. Vukan 'forgot the advice of his father' and believed that with the help of Hungary he could get control of Serbia. The establishment of a powerful Slav state in the Balkans, whether Serbian or Bulgarian, was contrary to the interests of Hungary, and support for Vukan was conditional on his accepting the Hungarian King as overlord. When Stephen had been driven from the country Imre adopted the title King of Serbia, seeking to bring the country under the control of Rome and asking for a crown for Vukan. Successful and final conversion of Serbia to the 'true Church' could be guaranteed if it were ruled by a loyal son of that Church.

In Serbia, however, Hungarian influence soon declined. Tsar Kalojan, concerned at the growing influence of Hungary, invaded the country with an army of Bulgarians and Kumans. As a result of the invasion the Serbians were compelled to give up Nish and the Hungarians Branichev, both towns becoming seats of Bulgarian bishoprics. As a consequence of the Bulgarian victory Vukan was driven from eastern Serbia and Stephen returned to the throne. Imre, involved in a war with his brother Andrew, was no longer in a position to support Vukan, or resist the restoration of Stephen; the former had no option but to cut his losses and make the best deal he could with his brother. Reconciliation was achieved through the efforts of the third brother, Sava, who returned from Mount Athos to Serbia for that purpose. After 1207 there is no further mention of Vukan.

Stephen took advantage of the rivalry between the two Greek states, Nicea and Epirus, which disputed the inheritance of the lost empire, to obtain an autocephalous church for Serbia, feeling the danger of being so near, and subject to the pressure from, the Archbishop of Ohrid, now under the control of Theodore, the powerful Despot of Epirus, and despatched his brother, Sava, to Nicea with the request which was duly granted by the Patriarch. The agreement to grant an archbishopric to Serbia must be seen as a political move by Nicea against Epirus. In addition to the creation of the archbishopric a number of new episcopates were created. The Archbishop of Ohrid protested, claiming that it was uncanonical to appoint as Archbishop, Sava, who had never been a bishop, and, since in his view, the Church in Serbia was under his jurisdiction, it lay with him and not Nicea to make ecclesiastical appointments.

Stephen entered into alliance with Theodore of Epirus which was cemented by the marriage of the son of the former with the daughter of the Despot. The alliance gave Stephen the support of one of the most powerful rulers in the Balkans, but it created a situation which would recur in Serbian history. Radislav slavishly followed the policy of Theodore and submitted all claims to the Archbishop of Ohrid. The position of the Church in Serbia was affected by the ecclesiastical repercussions between Epirus and Nicea which followed the coronation of Theodore. The Patriarch of Nicea was accused of usurping the authority of Ohrid by establishing an autocephalous church in Serbia and granting the title of Archbishop to Sava. In a letter to the latter, whom he pointedly addressed as monk, Chomatonos accused him of deserting his calling, and protested that the true bishop was in Ras, a dependency of the Church in Bulgaria, and hence the See of Ohrid.

Boril, the successor to Kalojan in Bulgaria, attempted to continue the policy of his predecessor of alliance with Nicea, but his defeat by the Emperor Henry forced him to abandon his plans and to renounce all claims to territories held by the Latins and Hungarians. An alliance, cemented by marriage between Henry and the niece of Boril led to joint action against Stephen to force him to hand over Strez, a Bulgarian traitor who had joined forces with the Serbian ruler, but who then changed sides and joined the alliance against Serbia despite a plea by Sava to remain faithful to Stephen. When Strez died (murdered?) his lands did not go either to Boril or Stephen; some were seized by the Latins in Salonika, some by the Despot of Epirus.

More dangerous for Serbia was the alliance between Henry and Andrew of Hungary, accompanied by the customary marriage alliance between Andrew and the niece of the Emperor. King and Emperor met at Nish, probably in 1215, where they summoned Stephen to join them. Stephen, probably suspecting the intentions of the two rulers of having designs against him and sharing his lands, insisted on meeting the King alone. The meeting took place at Ravno and lasted 12 days, at the end of which Stephen and Andrew joined the Emperor. The Emperor's attitude towards Stephen was distinctly cool; possibly he was aware of the domination which Byzantium had exercised over Serbia in the past and as successor to the Greek Emperor wished to revive this claim.

The powerful combination of Hungary and the Empire decided Stephen to seek allies among the dissident Latin states who had their own disagreements with the Emperor, and probably through the good offices of Dubrovnik, he entered into friendly relations with Venice through his marriage with the granddaughter of the Doge. On the death of Emperor Henry in 1216 one party favoured the Hungarian king to succeed him, but the majority opted for Peter of Courteney, brother-in-law of the first Latin Emperor. The new Emperor did not sail directly to Constantinople, but at the request of the Venetians attempted to capture the city of Drac before proceeding to his new capital via Epirus in the direction of Ohrid and Salonika. His defeat and death at the hands of Theodore made the latter the most powerful ruler in the East and virtually destroyed the power of the Latin Empire. In Bulgaria, Boril, without the support of the Franks, was unable to maintain his power and was defeated and blinded by John Asen who had returned from Russia. Andrew of Hungary made his long delayed trip to the Holy Land but returned to Hungary without any achievements to his credit. The absence of Andrew made it possible for Stephen to achieve his life's ambition; probably with the help of the Venetians he finally obtained a crown from Rome.

From a contemporary account we are told that after the departure of Andrew, in the same period 'eodem tempore' Stephen 'dominus Servie sive Rasie' called 'megajupanus' obtained a crown from Pope Honorius III, who sent a legate to Serbia to perform the coronation. The Doge, writing the history of his family, states that Stephen's wife, granddaughter of the Doge, induced him to renounce his 'heresy' whereupon the legate crowned him and his wife. According to another source Sava sent his pupil Methodius to ask for a crown and the coronation was carried out by Sava at Zic. The monk Theodosius, according to whom Sava performed the coronation, says nothing about Rome or the origin of the crown. Henceforth Stephen bore the title First Crowned (Prvovenchani). It was only to be expected that the King of Hungary on his return from the Holy Land should protest at the crowning of Stephen, since he claimed the crown of Serbia for himself. It appears, however, that Sava, an able diplomat, was able to reconcile Andrew or at least persuade him to accept the fait accompli. The danger of Hungarian intervention was not great and disappeared when the King was faced with a revolt in Hungary itself.

In April 1223 Theodore captured Salonika, the second capital of the Latins. Boniface's son sought help from Hungary. A Church Council at Arta, Theodore's capital, concluded unanimously that the liberator should be proclaimed as Emperor; the capital of the new empire was Salonika. His regents, with the titles of dukes and sebastors, Greek and Albanians, ruled the themes in Macedonia and Albania up to the Serbian border lying north of Arban, Debar and Skopje. In the east Theodore extended his power as far as Thrace.

Stephen found it politic to maintain friendly relations with the most powerful ruler in the Balkans. Earlier around 1216 he had intended that his son should marry a princess from Epirus but this plan was frustrated by the Church on grounds of consanguinity. However, as Theodore grew stronger he was less inclined to take account of the Church and the marriage between Radislav and his daughter was duly solemnised. Radislav as successor to Stephen was entrusted with the government of Duclea and perhaps

Trebinje. The old Hum was generally divided into two parts with two Great Zupans. According to one of the earliest sources, Orbino's History (itself probably based on a chronicle now lost), after the death of Nemanje's brother Miroslav, his widow and young son were driven out and one Peter proclaimed as ruler. Orbino further states that Stephen and his son defeated Peter near Mostar and confined his territories to the area between the Neretsa and Tsetinje; the lands south of the Neretsa were given by Stephen to his son.

Stephen followed the example of his father and died as a monk under the name of Simeon. Among his four sons Sava crowned Radislav as King, while Vladislav and Urosh probably received their own territories. The fourth son, Predislav, became a monk adopting the name of Sava, becoming Bishop of Hum and finally Archbishop of Serbia as Sava II (1263-70).

The reign of Radislav, who ruled from 1228-1234, was in sad contrast to that of his father. As a son and husband of the Byzantine royal house he aimed to be a Greek; politically he was entirely under the influence of his father-in-law and the Serbian Church was once more subordinate to the archbishopric of Ohrid, though in questions of liturgy it relied not on the Patriarch of Nicea but on the Archbishop of Epirus. The subservience of the Church was not approved by Sava who, taking advantage of the capture of Jerusalem by Frederick II, made a pilgrimage to the Holy Land.

The power of the Latin Empire continued to deteriorate, Baldwin II who now succeeded his brother Robert in 1288 was threatened by Epirus, Nicea and Bulgaria. The danger from Epirus was removed as a result of the defeat of Theodore at the hands of the Bulgarians under Tsar Asen II, in consequence of which the whole area west of Adrianople to Skopje, Ohrid and Drac was now in Bulgarian hands. Manuel, Theodore's brother, now ruled in Epirus while Theodore was a prisoner of the Bulgarians, but retained only Salonika, Thessaly and Epirus. The Senate of Dubrovnik, concerned over the future of trade in Drac and the surrounding area, hastened to acclaim Asen as 'Emperor of the Bulgarians and Greeks', in order to maintain their trading privileges. Meanwhile the relations between Bulgaria and Hungary broke down; in the war that followed Asen was able to capture Belgrade from the Hungarians, since this was one of the cities mentioned in his charter confirming the trading rights of Dubrovnik. Two years later, however, Belgrade was once more in Hungarian hands and under the ecclesiastical jurisdiction of the Bishop of Srem. The defeat of Theodore left Radislav dangerously exposed; Asen laid claim to the overlordship of Serbia and supported Vladislav against his brother. Radislav was overthrown and with his wife left Serbia and fled to Dubrovnik, where he was warmly welcomed, partly no doubt as a result of a promise of trading privileges to the merchants of the Republic if he should return to power. From there the fugitives sailed to Drac; later Radislav, without his wife, returned to Serbia to end his days as a monk.

Vladislav who ruled from 1234-1243 was more fortunate and an abler ruler than his brother, but was too much under the influence of Bulgaria. At the beginning of his reign relations with Dubrovnik were bad, probably due to the support which Radislav had received from the Republic. There appears to have been a plan to restore Radislav with the help of Dubrovnik; in a letter from Split to Dubrovnik the citizens of the former express great joy at the hoped for success of the Republic against Vladislav. If such a plan existed it never came to fruition, although more than a year was to pass before Dubrovnik was prepared to make peace with Vladislav.

The most significant event in the reign of Vladislav was the Mongol invasion which devastated Hungary, Bulgaria and to a lesser extent Serbia. Vladislav was unable to maintain himself in power and was forced to renounce the throne in favour of his younger brother Urosh, though retaining the title of King and some territories in Pomorje (the Littoral). The reasons for the overthrow of Vladislav are not known. Vladislav apparently went to Dubrovnik but the Republic was not willing to support him in any plan to recover the throne, since the Senate assured Urosh of their good intentions and negotiations began between the King and the Republic.

Urosh I who ruled from 1243-1276 was praised for his greatness by Danilo; this was standard practice for the latter for whom no Serbian ruler was less than perfect. In fact he was deficient in talent and vision which were such conspicuous features of his father. In foreign affairs he hesitated between the Greeks in Nicea and Epirus, Hungary and the new French rulers in Naples, Albania and Greece. He was at first linked with Nicea whose ruler, John Vatatzes, had seized all Bulgarian territory from Adrianople to the Vardar. Michael of Epirus occupied the territory west of the Vardar, including Veles, Prilep and Ohrid, but lost most of it to Nicea, now the most powerful state in the Balkans with territory stretching to the frontiers of Serbia. Clearly this was a potentially dangerous situation for Urosh.

The attempt to restore the power of Bulgaria led to an attack against Serbia, although the reasons for this attack are not clear; possibly Serbia was regarded as an ally of Nicea. Bulgaria was supported by Dubrovnik whose relations with Urosh for most of his reign were unfriendly. The Republic was concerned above all with extending its trade and territory. A further cause of friction arose over the control of the Church; the Pope had removed control of the archbishoprics in Bosnia from Dubrovnik – in compensation the hierarchy in Dubrovnik sought to gain control over the whole area of Bar in Serbian territory. In 1252 Urosh at the head of a large army appeared before the city, but after some delay offered peace. In the following year ambassadors from Bulgaria arrived in Dubrovnik proposing an alliance against Serbia. The Republic promised a naval attack against the Serbian coastal towns and agreed to hand over all the captured territory to Asen. In return the tsar promised to support the claims of the Church in the Republic and to grant trading privileges. In spite of an attack against Serbia which was more of a pillaging raid, peace was restored between Serbia and Bulgaria; Dubrovnik was isolated, having lost all ecclesiastical control in the Serbian lands.

The friendly relations between Urosh and Nicea from which the King had derived no advantage soon deteriorated. When Theodore Lascaris forced Michael of Epirus to cede the city of Drac, the Despot determined to resist and found ready allies – Villeharden, prince of Achea, and Manfred, King of Sicily. Urosh joined this alliance which was strengthened by his marriage (third?) with a French princess 'od plemene fruzska' according to Danilo. In consequence of his alliance with the West, relations with Hungary, now recovering its strength after the devastation of the Mongol invasion, and Serbia now improved. The Hungarian king, at war with Bulgaria, seized Vidin and advanced on Plevna and Trnovo. In 1261 relations were cemented by the marriage between Urosh's eldest son Dragutin and the daughter of the Hungarian king. One result of the rapprochment with Hungary was the acquisition of Hum. Resistance to the claims of the Hungarian king to the overlordship of Serbia, however, led Urosh to seek closer relations with the Greeks. But a much more dangerous opponent to Serbia and to Michael Palaeologus in the recaptured Constantinople now appeared in the person of Charles of Anjou who, in a victory over Manfred of Sicily, had deprived him of his crown and life.

In the following year Charles entered into negotiations with Baldwin, the titular Emperor, with the aim of restoring the Latin Empire, as a reward for which Charles would obtain any territory he might choose either in Epirus or 'In regnis Albania et Servie'. In view of this threat Urosh was forced to turn to the Emperor Michael who, faced with the prospect of an attack from the West, was anxious to have Serbia and Bulgaria on his side.

Disagreement over the respective claims to border territories hindered a Bulgarian-Byzantine alliance but Michael had more success with Urosh, and it was arranged that Milutin, the second son of the King, should marry Michael's daughter. The princess was already on her way to Serbia when the political situation was drastically altered by the crushing defeat which Urosh suffered at the hands of the Hungarians at Machva. Among the conditions of peace it appears that Urosh was forced to agree to share power with Dragutin, his eldest son; since the latter was the son-in-law of the

Hungarian king this would ensure a friendly Serbia from the point of view of Hungary. The war which ultimately broke out between Charles of Anjou and Michael did not involve Urosh.

The relations between Urosh and Dubrovnik had steadily deteriorated since the peace of 1254. In the course of the year 1266 an ambassador from the city sought the help of Venice against the Serbian king. There is preserved a letter from Urosh's wife Helen to the Prince and Archbishop of Dubrovnik, promising to inform them if her husband intended an attack on the city. In 1275 Urosh appeared at the head of an army before the city, destroying the houses and the vineyards outside the walls but making no direct attack. Meanwhile news came of the death of the Doge of Venice and an attack was expected by his son who was also Prince of Dubrovnik. (It was not unusual for the citizens of the Adriatic cities to request Venice to supply them with rulers.) He advanced into Serbian territory but peace was signed between Serbia and Dubrovnik through the mediation of Venice. The promise made by Urosh after the battle of Machva had not been fulfilled. Dragutin, supported by Louis of Hungary, overthrew his father who retired to Hum as a monk, and Dragutin was crowned King.

Dragutin and Milutin

The rapid development of Serbia under the brothers Dragutin and Milutin was aided by the growth of economic power as a result of the exploitation of the Serbian mines through the introduction of German miners or Saxons as they were known. The wealth resulting from the output of these mines increased the military power at the disposal of the Serbian rulers, enabling them for instance to hire foreign mercenaries. In contrast to the growing Serbian power the Empire continued on its inexorable decline.

Stephen Dragutin did not long reign as King of Serbia. He established the Queen Mother, Helen, as ruler of the coastal areas, which were long known as the territories of the Queen, while it is likely that his younger brother received his own lands. The ancient hostility with Dubrovnik was forgotten and Dragutin maintained friendly relations with the Republic, while he found it expedient to keep on good terms with Charles of Anjou. The Emperor Michael, in order to strengthen his position against the threat from the West, had been conducting negotiations with the Pope over the question of Church unity. Negotiations broke down on the accession to the Holy See of the Frenchman Martin IV, a protegé of Charles, who saw in a union of the Churches a hindrance to his own plans for the restoration of the Latin power in Constantinople. Charles began an offensive in Albania but suffered a complete defeat at the hands of Michael, a victory vividly described by Marino Sanudo in his 'Istoria del regno di Romania'. As a result of the victory 'il detto castello dello Gianina (Canino) che e in la Vallona e Duraccio fu restituto all imperator de Greci predetto'.

The leaders of Charles' army were taken to Constantinople where they remained 'molti anni'. Charles now entered into negotiations with Venice which promised troops and ships for an attack on Constantinople in the following spring and the establishment as Emperor of Philip, the son of Baldwin II, who was also the son-in-law of Charles. Michael took countermeasures from the West; through the intermediary of Genoa he concluded a secret alliance with Peter of Aragon, son-in-law of the unfortunate Manfred. In Sicily a rising against the French known as the Sicilian Vespers destroyed all the plans Charles had prepared for the conquest of Constantinople.

In about 1282 Dragutin suffered a fall from his horse and broke his leg; this the King saw as a punishment for his action against his father, and he yielded or in the words of Danilo made a gift of the crown to his brother Milutin. The abdication took place at a Council at the town of Dedzev, but there is a certain amount of confusion about the circumstances and what was decided there. According to one source, Dragutin, during the lifetime of his father, had suffered some misfortune. This clearly could not refer to his fall, which occurred after the death of his father. Being unfitted for power therefore he renounced the throne in favour of his young brother Milutin. Danilo speaks of events which forced Dragutin to give up his powers but though he speaks of disturbances he does not specify what they were, and makes no mention of Milutin's involvement, nor of his presence at court during these disturbances. William Adams, an unreliable witness, considered Milutin only as regent for his nephew, Dragutin's son; according to his version Naples, Venice and the Pope always referred to Dragutin as 'rex Servie', the only legitimate ruler of the kingdom. Adam's view cannot be accepted. He states that Urosh (Milutin) rebelled against Dragutin 'Urosius contra jam factus regem Stefanum Dragutin insurrexit quem Stefano bello agrediens superavit' but having defeated him he 'cum eo voluntatie condivisit'.

If this is an accurate account of what happened it is difficult to understand why Dragutin, having defeated his brother, should then have agreed to divide the kingdom. The alleged revolt of Milutin against his brother has not been confirmed from any other source. There is also some confusion regarding the lands which Dragutin retained for himself. According to one source Dragutin retained enough lands for himself. Two years after his renunciation of the throne Dragutin obtained lands in the north beyond the frontiers of the Serbian state, which Danilo explicitly states as being part of the Hungarian and Bosnian lands, and which included Belgrade, Machva and north-east Bosnia, to be held as a vassal of the King of Hungary. Danilo states that immediately after handing over power Dragutin went to his own territories in the place called Machva given him by his father-in-law the King of Hungary. Strictly interpreted this would suggest that Dragutin had received Machva before his abdication, but we know from other evidence that he could only have received Machva after 1284. Danilo is also misleading when he describes Dragutin as King of all the 'Serbian and Pomorski and Podunavski and Sremski lands'. In view of these errors Danilo must be considered an unreliable witness.

The account of events given by an Anonymous Traveller is equally misleading; he considered Ras as being divided into two parts – Ras in the strict sense of the word, where Milutin ruled, and Serbia where Dragutin ruled. That these lands were one before the rule of Milutin is clearly stated when the traveller speaks of the relationship between the two brothers. 'In hoc regnum fuit semper unus rex sed nunc sunt duo reges; unus regnans in Rassia et hic est maior et vocatus Urosius – hoc enim nomine vocantur omnes regis Rassie, alter vocatus Stephanus et hic regnat in Servie qui est parte Ungarie.' Both these kings are brothers but the eldest Stephen is King of Serbia who 'post mortem patris' reigned in both parts for two years. Danilo from whom we might expect a clear and accurate account of events, avoids speaking of the essential negotiations. From the words he attributes to Dragutin on that occasion it can be stated with certainty that Milutin accepted the crown for life.

According to the Anonymous Traveller Dragutin handed over power unconditionally, renouncing the throne not only for himself – with which all sources are in agreement – but also for his heirs. If it was clear that Milutin was to rule during his lifetime, it was not known what decision was reached regarding the succession after his death. Adams considers the accession of Milutin as an act of usurpation and regards the son of Dragutin, Vladislav, as the rightful heir. He further states that after the division of the lands Dragutin was the main king. More reliable evidence can be found from a portrait of Milutin, Dragutin and his wife Katerina; above the head of Milutin are the words 'Stephen Urosh King of all the Serbian lands and the Littoral' (vse Srpski zemli i pomorski) while Dragutin is simply described as King and first founder of the church, 'Stephen kralj i prvi ktitor'. In the same church there is an inscription 'in the days of the young King Urosh – King of all the Serbian lands and King Stephen brother of King Urosh'. The term 'young king' usually referred to the heir during his father's lifetime. Here, however, the words 'young king' refer to the fact that Milutin was the younger brother and not to his subordination to Dragutin. While in foreign sources Dragutin is referred to as King, there is no reliable evidence that he bore this title after his abdication; in the lands he ruled, however, he would be King.

From a study of the conflicting evidence it seems clear that Dragutin handed over power to Milutin not only on account of his accident but because of some disorder. What these disorders were we do not know. One possible answer may lie with the nobility. An important consequence of the rise of the Serbian state in its long struggle against the Byzantine Empire was the emergence of the 'great men' (velika vlastela) whose representatives governed the provinces and who intervened decisively in the affairs of State. The Nemanje dynasty itself had developed from the Zupa; the success of the first Nemanje in creating a strong state had been due in the first place to the support of the nobles, and the successors of Nemanje met with fierce opposition when they attempted to increase the power of the monarchy. When Milutin gained power in 1282 a large number of nobles, obviously dissatisfied with Dragutin, transferred their allegiance to his brother. The role of the Church was equally important. When Sava organised the Serbian Church he offered to the central power the model of a hierarchy which developed rapidly in the 13th century, constantly at the service of the dynasty from which its founder had sprung.

An independent Church was only possible as part of a strong state, and was therefore opposed to the interests of the great nobles. In addition to the latter there existed a group of lesser men 'male vlastela' who aspired to take part in the civil and military administration of the State, and for whom a strong state was a safeguard against the ambitions of the over-powerful subjects. A king who lacked the will to limit the ambitions of the great men and appeared incapable of restricting their power would be unacceptable to the lesser men and to the Church. It was logical, therefore, that they would try to replace him by another member of the dynasty. Dragutin's policy seemed to confirm their fears. To his mother he had granted huge territories on the coast between Dubrovnik and Skadar, where she ruled with her own army and the power to contract treaties in her own name, a policy which could be seen as a weakening of the State, particularly in view of her western sympathies. It is possible that this encouraged hopes among the great men of carving out autonomous provinces for themselves, and led to fears among the lesser men and the Church whose fate was linked with a strong state. In view of the fact that Milutin was seen as the defender of the State, and was strengthened by the sympathy and support of the army, he demanded power. Dragutin and his supporters, fearing war, supported a compromise acceptable to Milutin, and Dragutin's abdication must be seen as the result of pressure rather than a voluntary act.

When Milutin came to power the war between the Angevins and Michael Palaeologus was at its height. The allies, Franks, Serbia and Thessaly began an attack, unaware of the rising against the French in Sicily. Milutin seized the city of Skopje, now lost for ever to the Empire. Michael was preparing an attack against Thessaly and Serbia with the object of making Milutin his vassal; in the midst of these preparations, however, Michael died in 1282. Milutin took full advantage of the accelerated decline of the Empire under Andronicus II who succeeded his father. An attack by a combined force of Greeks and Tartars against Serbia was repelled; Milutin and Dragutin co-operated in a campaign in eastern Macedonia where they advanced as far as Porec, Kicevo and Debar in western Macedonia. Serbia benefited from the friendly relations which had been maintained with Bulgaria, whose ruler George Terter was the father-in-law of Milutin. The hostility existing between Serbia and Byzantium and the influence of the Queen Mother raised hopes in Rome that Serbia might be brought into union with the Catholic Church. Many attempts were made by the Papacy to bring the Queen Mother and Dragutin into union but the summons to Milutin to adhere to Rome had no effect. When Helen made her visit to Bulgaria the Pope at her request sent a letter to 'Georgius imperator Bulgarorum' to win him over to Rome.

It was fortunate that the situation in Bulgaria diverted the attention of Milutin. Terter was forced to become the vassal of the Tartar Nogaj and give his daughter to the son of the latter, Chag, who thus became the brother-in-law of Milutin's wife. But the weakness of Terter's position encouraged the boyars in a struggle for independence. In the west round Branichev two brothers, Drman and Kudelin at the head of a mixed force of Bulgarians, Kumans and Tartars carried out a pillaging raid into Hungary and the territory of Dragutin. In Vidin the ruler Prince Shishman was linked with the Kumans. Terter's brother-in-law ruled in the central area, while three brothers, Smil or Smilep, Radoslav and Voisil occupied part of Montenegro. Unable to resist any longer the pressure from the Tartars, Terter fled to Byzantine territory and was succeeded by Smil, a puppet of the Tartar Nogaj. Milutin took advantage of the weakness and unrest in Bulgaria to launch an offensive against Drman and Kudelin, and after a successful campaign Branichev was annexed to the territories of Dragutin. In order to take revenge against Serbia, Shishman, with a combined force of Bulgarians and Tartars appeared unexpectedly before Zic, obviously with the intention of pillaging the archbishopric, but was forced to withdraw without any success. Milutin then turned to deal with Shishman and seized Vidin; Shishman fled across the Danube but soon made his peace with Serbia.

The Tartar ruler Nogaj considered the advance of the Serbians to Branichev as a violation of his rights as supreme ruler of Bulgaria, and sent a mixed force of Kumans, Tartars and Christians from the Caucasus against Serbia, but his feelings were apparently soothed by the despatch of an ambassador from Milutin. The King promised to remain at peace with

Bulgaria and sent his son Stephen as hostage. Nogaj had now more serious matters to worry about; in a struggle for power within the Golden Horde he was killed in 1299 thus making it possible for Stephen to escape and return to his native land. On his return he was married to Theodora, daughter of the Bulgarian ruler Smil, and became regent for his father in Zeta and the Littoral which prior to this had been ruled by his grandmother Helen.

In Hungary the murder of Louis IV was followed by a struggle for the succession between the last Arped and the House of Anjou. Charles II based his claim on the ground that he was the husband of Maria, the sister of Louis. In 1292 his son Charles Martel was proclaimed King; a similar claim could be made by Dragutin, who was also brother-in-law of Louis, but he appears not to have pressed it, and to have supported Charles. His adherence to the Angevin cause is confirmed by a charter of Charles in which Dragutin's son 'vir magnifcius' is granted possession of the dukedom of Slavonia, and is married to Constantia, granddaughter of the Duke of Slavonia, Albertin. When the son of Charles Martel was striving to obtain the Hungarian crown, the King of Naples, Charles of Anjou, recommended him to Dragutin and his wife Catherina.

Meanwhile after 20 years of fighting the situation on the Serbo-Byzantine border had become unacceptable to the Empire. The Emperor was advised to make peace with Serbia in view of the critical situation in Asia Minor arising from the Turkish threat. No less than five attempts were made to negotiate terms. Milutin stipulated that all towns captured from the Empire during the course of the war must remain in Serbian hands and the peace should be confirmed by a marriage between Milutin and Eudokia, sister of Andronicus. There were difficulties to be overcome before such a marriage could take place; Milutin was already married – indeed he had been married four times – the current wife being the daughter of the Bulgarian Terter. Like all marriages this union had been entered into for political reasons at a time when Bulgarian power seemed dangerous to Serbia. With the decline in Bulgarian power Milutin now found his wife boring; the legality of the marriage was in any case doubtful. Milutin welcomed the idea of a marriage into the Byzantine royal house. The second difficulty came from the proposed bride herself who refused the offer, thus threatening the peace negotiations. When Milutin was informed of the rejection of his offer of marriage he threatened the Emperor with a renewal of hostilities. Faced with the prospect of a renewed war for which the Empire was quite unprepared, the Emperor was obliged to sacrifice his daughter Simonides.

Within Serbia the peace with Byzantium was opposed by the party of the great men who had derived material benefits from the border warfare. This opposition was strengthened by both sons of the sebastocrat John of Thessaly who were willing to conclude an alliance with Serbia against the

Emperor, and by Bulgaria where the widow of Smil had promised her hand to Milutin with the prospect of a union of the crowns of Serbia and Bulgaria. In Constantinople the marriage of Simonides with Milutin was opposed on the grounds that his marriage with Anna was legal, and secondly that Simonides was below marriageable age; the marriage nevertheless took place. The friendly relations which resulted from this marriage were a contributory factor in extending Byzantine influence in the country. Byzantine customs were introduced in the Serbian court and there now began that Byzantinisation of Serbian life which reached its peak in the half Greek government of Stephen Dushan. It is true of course that the political situation changed, and Serbia fought many wars against the Empire, but paradoxically as Serbia extended its territory at the expense of the Empire, Byzantine influence and culture became stronger.

Lasting peace, however, was not possible between Serbia and the Empire unless Milutin was prepared to renounce his territorial ambitions, apart from the fact that the nobles were opposed to peace which would deprive them of the advantages they had derived from the war. Feeling, perhaps, that more could be gained by co-operation with the West, Milutin concluded an alliance with Charles with the object of restoring the Latin Empire. Milutin promised to adhere to the Catholic Church and to cement the alliance by the marriage of his daughter with the younger son of the titular Emperor. Charles for his part bound himself to aid Milutin except against his cousin Philip of Tarento. So far as territorial claims were concerned Skopje and Polog were excluded from discussion; Charles as Emperor granted to Milutin, Ovecpol, the territory between Prosek and Prilep, the area of Kichevo up to the borders of Ohrid. The alliance directed against Byzantium seems not to have changed the relationship between Milutin and Andronicus; in May 1306 Andronicus at the request of his 'son' Milutin confirmed the donation made by the King to the monastery of St. Nicholas at Skopje, that is, in Serbian territory, which does not suggest a climate of hostility between them.

Preparations were put in train for the admission of Milutin to the Catholic Church. The Pope in effect legalised the position of the King's young son Stephen. Whatever the motives of Milutin were over the question of his adherence to Rome, it aroused opposition within his own state. If, as is likely, his negotiations with the Pope and his alliance with Charles of Valois were undertaken in the hope of gaining political advantage, they proved to be disappointing. A Serbian attack against the frontiers of the Empire failed. Meanwhile Catherine, the wife of Charles through whom he based his claim to the Empire died, and all his plans had to be abandoned, since he could no longer rely on the support of the Venetians whom the Pope had anathemised because of their attack on Ferrara. Milutin therefore turned once more to co-operation with Byzantium.

After the marriage of Milutin and Simonides relations with Dragutin worsened; though the reasons are not clear, there is no doubt that the deterioration was bound up with the plans of Byzantium over the succession to the crown of Serbia. The Empress Irene had ambitions for her sons Demetrius and Theodore, and the refusal of Andronicus to share power with them led her to look elsewhere, and she left the capital for Salonika. In view of the fact that the marriage between Milutin and Simonides (who was certainly not more than seven when the marriage took place) was not likely to produce children, Irene hoped for the succession of her sons. When Milutin visited his mother-in-law the matter was discussed between them. Demetrius visited Serbia and was warmly welcomed by his sister, but the visit was short; neither the people nor the country was to his liking and he quickly departed. Theodore, on the other hand, succeeding to the dukedom of Montferrat, preferred the certainty of Montferrat and the delights of Italy to the doubtful prospects of Serbia.

We do not know what promises were made by Milutin regarding the succession; in any case this was a matter on which Dragutin felt very strongly, and war broke out between the brothers. The war appears to have started in 1301 and Milutin seems to have been successful. The town of Rudnik lies in Srem; in 1296 therefore it lay in the territory of Dragutin. In the plans drawn up by Milutin, Rudnik is included in his territory. Much of the evidence we have about the war comes from Dubrovnik; merchants complain of their inability to carry out instructions from the city because of the war, and this can only refer to the internal struggle between Milutin and Dragutin. The civil war in Serbia could not remain a purely internal matter given the links which both brothers had with foreign powers. Dragutin was deterred from attacking his brother because of the support Milutin was receiving from Byzantium, or rather which he hoped to receive. In the event the support failed to materialise owing partly to the Turkish threat and the war with Venice. Milutin therefore turned once more to the West and entered into negotiations with Charles of Valois and the Pope in 1308.

While Milutin was endeavouring to strengthen his links with the West, and managing to maintain reasonably friendly relations with the Empire, apart from some border skirmishes, Dragutin was drawn into the internal struggle in Hungary, and found himself in open conflict with Charles of Anjou, placing him in the position of having to fight on two fronts. Worse, Hungary on whom alone he could rely for help against Milutin was in fact working for the latter. This was the result of an attempt of one group in Hungary to make Dragutin king through his links with the Arpads. The offer of the crown was made, but in Catholic eyes it was claimed that a marriage celebrated under the rites of the Orthodox Church could not provide an heir to the crown of Hungary. According to the account of the

Anonymous Traveller 'rex Ungeria motrius sine heredi – ac etiam sorores eius omnesfuerunt nupte scismaticis'.

Dragutin's aim was to drive his brother from the throne and install his own son Vladislav as King. All the great men joined Dragutin presumably for the same reasons as they had abandoned him before; fear of a strong central state under Milutin who now found himself isolated. He was saved by the support he received from the Church which had remained constant throughout, and the money he obtained enabled him to recruit foreign troops, Tartars and Turks, and to re-establish his authority in Serbia.

What was the attitude of the Queen Mother to the fratricidal strife in Serbia? Helen herself was ruler of the coastal areas and could not be indifferent to events. Much of the information we have regarding the Queen comes from the life of Danilo. Danilo writes of the 'bitter words' she expressed and describes her as cursing Dragutin when he rose against his father and drove him from the throne. Helen, however, seems to have forgiven her son, and for the rest of her life her sympathies lay more with Dragutin than with Milutin; nor was this simply on the grounds that Milutin had forced his brother to renounce the throne. She was opposed to the pro-Byzantine policy of Milutin, seeing in it the cause of the quarrel between her sons, into which she was bound to be drawn. In 1309 Milutin's son Stephen replaced his grandmother in the Littoral and Helen retired to a monastery built for her by Milutin.

According to Danilo hostilities between the two brothers ended in 1313; this date can be confirmed if we take into account the fact that Dragutin was preparing an attack in Hungary, suggesting that his position in his own country was now secure. In addition relations between Milutin and Venice were becoming closer against their common enemy the Ban of Bosnia. It is possible that the brothers reconciled their differences at the beginning of the year. Furthermore, twice that year Milutin sent help to the Emperor against the Turks, suggesting an end to the civil war in Serbia. Little can be said of the negotiations between Milutin and Dragutin. According to Adams, Milutin revolted against his brother and was defeated, but Dragutin, unwilling to shed his brother's blood, voluntarily agreed to a division of territory. On the death of Dragutin his son should succeed him in his own lands, but Milutin, while he continued to rule in his own lands, would do so as a vassal of Vladislav the son of Dragutin. This account does not square with the facts. There can be no doubt that the real victor was Milutin and this was recognised by Dragutin; in a charter granted to the monastery of Banja, Dragutin gave Milutin the full customary title and describes himself as 'brother of the great King Urosh (Milutin)'.

In 1314 the Queen Mother died and an attempt was made by a group of nobles to expel Milutin and establish in Zeta his son Stephen. On the failure of this coup, the nobles submitted under 'very favourable conditions' but orders were given that Stephen should be blinded, though, judging from later events, this does not seem to have been carried out successfully. According to Adams the person entrusted with the task 'corruptuus pecuniae' did not carry out the order, and the prince was able to see 'a little'. After this Stephen, along with his wife and two sons, was banished to Constantinople where they remained for some years in an imperial palace in friendly relations with Andronicus II. Later, probably through the influence of the monks of Hilander and the Archbishop Nicodemus, father and son were reconciled; the family returned to Serbia and Stephen was granted rule over the Zupa of Zeta.

The last years of Dragutin were spent in peace, but if fighting had ceased, friendly relations between the brothers could not last. The basic question on which the negotiations had closed, namely the succession, could not be decided in a manner satisfactory to both sides. Dragutin's main aim was to ensure the succession of his son as King, and with this object in view he strove to regularise his relations with Hungary – the only power on whom he could rely – before Charles Robert consolidated his throne and overcame his enemies. Thus Dragutin, who at the beginning of August 1313 had been preparing an attack on Hungary, became reconciled with Charles Robert. In 1316 he died having previously become a monk. The course of events after his death is known only from foreign sources; Adams states that after the death of his brother Milutin put down a revolt by Vladislav, but we do not know what the word revolt means in this context. It is not disputed that from 1282 Dragutin had his own territories; if it was agreed in the negotiations between the two brothers in 1313 that Vladislav should succeed his father in the lands held by Dragutin – the view expressed by Adams – then Vladislav's succession could not be regarded as a revolt. Only if Vladislav laid claim to all the Serbian lands could his actions be regarded as rebellion. It is more likely that Milutin intended on Dragutin's death to incorporate his brother's lands into his own state. On the failure of the revolt Vladislav was imprisoned and remained in captivity during the lifetime of Milutin.

Much more dangerous was the quarrel between Milutin and Charles Robert of Hungary; the latter, having overcome his enemies, sought from Milutin the lands which Dragutin had held from the Hungarian crown. The war between the two powers was fought in various areas from the Danube to Albania, and involved the Ban of Bosnia. The latter attempted to bring under his control the coastal towns, but this affected the Venetians with whom his relations were bad. At the same time Charles Robert transferred his whole army towards the Sava and fixed his camp on the banks of the river between Kolubar and Belgrade, taking the latter town by storm. From the point of view of Charles the occupation of the lands of Dragutin by Milutin was an act of usurpation. 'Belgrade under Milutin's rule was a very different thing from Belgrade under the rule of Dragutin.' Moreover, military action against Milutin could be justified on the grounds that the Serbian monarch was interfering in the internal affairs of Hungary by supporting the opponents of Charles. Milutin sought to obtain a marriage between his son and the daughter of Ladislav, the pretender to the Hungarian throne; this, however, was strongly opposed by the Papal legate and the project fell through without threatening the alliance between Milutin and the party opposed to Charles.

Charles was aiming at more than a regularisation of the territorial question and sought allies on all sides. In the war against Milutin he obtained the support of the Ban of Bosnia and in Albania of Philip of Tarento. His position was strengthened by the support of the Pope, who was particularly active in Albania stirring up the enemies of Milutin. However, action on such a wide scale with allies who did not have a common interest in the outcome of the fight did not achieve the desired results. The most successful action was achieved by Charles who went over to the offensive in 1319. Despite the capture of Shapats and Belgrade, achieved only with great difficulty by the Hungarian armies, Milutin was able to maintain his southern borders, and now began to call himself King of Albania, and peace was quickly restored.

Milutin lived long enough to see the outbreak of the war between Andronicus II and his grandson, the future Andronicus III, the son of Michael who had been crowned by his father but died in 1320. As a result of the behaviour of the young Andronicus, relations with his grandfather deteriorated to the point where civil war broke out between them. Fighting involved outside powers, notably Serbia and Bulgaria, as well as Venice and Genoa. Intervention in Byzantine affairs offered an opportunity to extend the frontiers in the south as an alternative to expansion in the north-east, where Serbia was faced with the power of the Angevins of Naples, and the threat from the Despot of Epirus. The internal unrest in Hungary weakened the effectiveness of the anti-Serbian alliance, but it led to closer relations with Byzantium, partly due to the efforts of Simonides, who acted as intermediary between her husband and her father. Consequently Milutin was well informed about the situation in the Empire. In 1320 he sent word to Andronicus II demanding the return of some 2,000 troops which he had provided for the use of the Emperor, while at the same time entering into negotiations with the younger Andronicus. The fact that Serbia did not provide Andronicus with armed assistance may have been due to the death of Milutin in 1321 and the influence of Simonides who, adhering to her father, hindered the despatch of troops.

The death of Milutin was followed by a period of unrest in Serbia arising from the rival claims to the throne. There were three main claimants; Constantin the eldest son of Milutin; Vladislav the son of Dragutin, who had been imprisoned by Milutin on the death of his father and freed on the latter's death, and Stephen the second son of Milutin, whom his father ordered to be blinded but who appears to have escaped this fate. Constantin was proclaimed as King in Zeta; in Skadar he minted his own coinage and is seen seated on the throne with crown and sceptre. Constantin enjoyed only limited support. In the north his rival Vladislav, on his release from prison, was welcomed in those territories his father had ruled as lawful ruler. But of the three claimants, the one who finally succeeded was Stephen, although he seemed to have the least prospect of success; the news that he was not blind spread throughout the country, and this 'miracle' was seen as a sign of God's grace. Adams, who was a bitter enemy of Stephen, claims that he had never been blinded and retained some of his sight but had hidden this from his father.

The situation now existing between Stephen and Constantin could only be resolved by war. Constantin rejected Stephen's offer to divide the lands and claimed that Stephen had no right to rule. Stephen was crowned in 1322 along with his young son Stephen as co-ruler or 'mlada kralj'. Constantin was defeated and killed and the young King was entrusted with the government of Zeta. Stephen had more difficulty with his cousin Vladislav, probably because of the help the latter received from Charles Robert of Hungary and the Ban Stephen of Bosnia. War between them continued until 1324 when Vladislav was defeated and fled to Hungary where he remained until his death. One result of the internal struggle in Serbia was the final loss of Hum to Bosnia; all further attempts on the part of Serbia to recover it proved vain.

While the war with Vladislav was going on, Stephen attempted to establish friendly relations with the Angevins of Naples, and on the death of his wife Theodora, he sought a marriage with Blanche, the daughter of Philip of Tarento in 1323. At the same time he expressed his readiness to enter into union with the Catholic Church, probably to forestall the claims of Vladislav. The Pope sent a legate to Serbia to carry out the negotiations. The proposed marriage was enthusiastically supported by Dubrovnik.

Negotiations over the marriage broke down, however, possibly because the Angevins considered Vladislav to be the rightful heir to the crown of Serbia, and Stephen ultimately married Maria Palaeologus, the niece of Simonides. One result of the marriage was to involve Serbia more directly in the civil war between Andronicus and his grandson. During the period of the third and final civil war in the Empire Stephen supported the old Emperor. Consequently relations between Stephen and the young

Andronicus were bad. The secret treaty arranged between them had produced no practical benefits; from the beginning of his reign Andronicus III pursued an anti-Serbian policy. In the course of the war Serbian troops besieged Ohrid but were forced to withdraw when Andronicus sent help to the beleagured city, and drove the Serbian troops from some neighbouring forts before retiring to Thrace. Andronicus found an ally in the person of Tsar Michael of Bulgaria, who abandoned his Serbian wife to marry the sister of Andronicus. The war between the Byzantine rulers was in one sense a war between Serbia and Bulgaria, each hoping to profit from the struggle. Both sides employed mercenaries; Stephen took Spanish and perhaps German troops into his service while Michael had Tartars and received help from Basaraba, Prince of the Vlachs a few months before the latter defeated Charles Robert of Hungary in 1330.

Bulgaria and Byzantium opened their attack on Serbia, but lack of co-ordination led to failure, and the Bulgarians were completely defeated at the Battle of Velbuzd, which destroyed the power of Bulgaria and eliminated the country as a serious rival to Serbia. Stephen then turned his attention to Andronicus III. When the latter was informed of the Bulgarian catastrophe the proposed advance on Serbia was abandoned, Andronicus preferring to take advantage of the disorders in Bulgaria following the defeat, seizing the towns of Mesembra and Diampol. Stephen drove the Emperor's troops from his borders, then triumphantly returned from the south to his own lands. The triumph of Stephen is commemorated by the monastery of Decani which was built in the course of the war, and from which Stephen acquired the name Decanski by which he is remembered.

In contrast to the successes against Bulgaria and Byzantium, the fighting in Bosnia resulted in losses for Serbia; the Bosnians extended their rule from the Neretsa to the borders of Dubrovnik. From this period up to 1378, Dubrovnik lay on the Serbian-Bosnian frontier. North of Dubrovnik only Ston remained to Serbia with the island of Mlet, which did not long remain in Serbian hands. In 1327 war broke out between Serbia and Dubrovnik. The cause of the war is not clear but may possibly have been linked with the support which the Republic had offered to Vladislav in his fight with Stephen. At the end of 1324 ambassadors were sent from Dubrovnik to Venice and to Serbia, both with the same commission – to resolve the differences with Stephen. At the same time the Senate decided unanimously, the Venetian dissenting, that the city should be closed to all foreigners, and that the transport of goods to Serbia should be forbidden unless the Senate decreed otherwise. The Venetians objected that they could not be treated like other foreigners, but were prepared, subject to this proviso, to support the embargo against Serbia. When Johannes de Caldarario was sent by Stephen to Dubrovnik he was warmly welcomed by the Senate who tried to convince him that they wanted peace. However, this diplomatic mission did not lead to an improvement in the relations between Serbia and Dubrovnik.

The Senate despatched an embassy to Venice to put before the Doge complaints 'de enormis et illicitis extortionibus nobis factis – per dominum regem Vrossium (Stephen) et gentium suam'. The aim of the embassy was to persuade the Venetians to forbid their citizens to travel or export goods to Kotor or other coastal towns belonging to Serbia. In return the Senate was prepared to make concessions. It was clear that the Republic was anxious to regulate its relations with Serbia, and the support of Venice might be decisive. The Venetians for their part entered into negotiations with Stephen, who was anxious to find a way of allowing Venetian goods into Serbia, but the latter were not prepared to co-operate unless the merchants of Dubrovnik had the trading privileges, previously enjoyed by them in the lands of the King, restored. In 1325, therefore, Venetian goods were forbidden to enter Serbia. The attitude of Venice towards Dubrovnik was quite definite; they supported the latter and informed Stephen that they did not intend to desert the Republic. According to earlier historians the differences between Serbia and Dubrovnik were finally settled by March 1326 when Stephen recognised and confirmed the rights and privileges of Dubrovnik merchants in Serbian territory. 'In 1326 in the city of Danj peace was restored between Dubrovnik and Stephen.' This statement can no longer be accepted; one month after the alleged restoration of peace there is evidence of unrest and fear in Dubrovnik of a war with Serbia. At the same time the Venetians continued diplomatic activity to arbitrate between Dubrovnik and Stephen.

The Senate of Dubrovnik gave a detailed account of the difficulties they had encountered in Serbia not only at the present but in the time of Stephen's father, although the latter had made peace with the Republic. Bearing in mind the persecution of the Dubrovnik merchants in Serbia, while the latter was at peace with the Republic, its traders had good reason to fear the consequences for them in time of war. What Dubrovnik wanted was compensation for the seizure of goods and a guarantee of future protection. However, it was made clear that Venice was only prepared to negotiate with Serbia on behalf of Dubrovnik if the latter were prepared to accede to Venetian demands.

The breakdown of the negotiations with Stephen led to a demand from Dubrovnik that Venice should act against Serbia. Three months after the meeting at Danj the Republic was resigned to war with Serbia. It is true that their position was strengthened by an alliance with the Ban of Bosnia, but the danger from Serbia was increasing, a danger all the greater in that it could threaten the interests of the merchants and consequently the interests of Dubrovnik itself. The Venetians were more willing to give promises of help than to fulfil them. A year after Dubrovnik had accepted the conditions under which Venice would provide help against Serbia, the Senate were still asking that the Venetian merchants should be withdrawn from Serbia.

War broke out between Serbia and Dubrovnik probably in the spring of 1327. It affected the relations between the latter and the citizens of Zadar, centering on the question whether the citizens of that city, subjects of Venice, had the right to maintain links with Serbia at a time when Venice was supporting Dubrovnik against the latter. The war came to an end in 1328, after which the trading privileges of the merchants of Dubrovnik were renewed and confirmed within the territories of Stephen Decanski.

In 1330 a quarrel broke out between Stephen and his son Dushan, a situation which had occurred frequently in the past between father and son. The King had another son from his second marriage, and although the latter was still a boy, Stephen proposed to make him joint ruler with Dushan, leading to jealousy and mistrust. Dushan enjoyed great popularity because of the part he had played in the wars of his father and in particular for his achievement at the Battle of Velbuzd. Dushan later claimed that 'evilly disposed persons' were attempting to influence his father to deprive him of his inheritance. In spite of a plea that father and son should live in peace, fighting broke out between them. After a period of open war interrupted by negotiations Stephen Decanski was finally defeated and imprisoned, dying shortly after, probably murdered. In September 1331 Dushan was crowned King.

CHAPTER II

The Serbian Empire

THE SITUATION IN THE BALKANS on the accession of Dushan was particularly favourable to Serbia; the crushing defeat inflicted on Bulgaria at the Battle of Velbuzd had eliminated that state as a serious rival, while the civil war in the Empire between Andronicus II and his grandson was an inducement to Dushan to intervene for his own advantage. In addition the Empire was under threat from the Turks in Asia Minor. Consequently Dushan's first offensive was directed against the territories of the Empire; within three years he had conquered the western half of Macedonia. The towns of Macedonia were not strongly garrisoned, and included Slavs who were unlikely to offer strong resistance, particularly in view of the inability of the Emperor to provide adequate protection. However, the relatively speedy and easy conquests of Dushan were due in part to the ensuing anarchy within the Empire arising from the civil war and hostility to John Cantacuzene. One of the leaders of the Serbian army, Sirgian, was a renegade who, having fled from Constantinople after being involved in a plot against Cantacuzene, offered his services to Dushan. Prior to this Dushan had succeeded in gaining control of Ohrid, Prilep and Strumnits; to these Sirgian added Kostor, thus extending further the military power of Serbia.

The civil war had accelerated a movement within the Empire towards greater autonomy on the part of the governors of the remote provinces. Sirgian urged Dushan to take advantage of this movement and advised him to seize Salonika, the second city of the Empire. The situation in Macedonia was particularly favourable for the Serbian advance; class antagonisms were becoming more bitter and were particularly acute in Salonika where a radical group known as the Zealots had seized power from the Aristocrats. The danger to the Empire came as much from Sirgian as from Dushan; the latter was seen as just another ambitious ruler casting covetous eyes on Byzantine territory – he might be defeated or reconciled. Sirgian was a dangerous example to other dissidents who could encourage anarchy and threaten the capital. If he could not be bought he must be killed.

Andronicus III meanwhile appeared before Salonika with a small army and shortly afterwards Sirgian was killed. Sirgian's death while removing a potential threat to the Empire, deprived Dushan of an important ally. Consequently he was prepared, since he had no immediate prospects of further military success, to accept Andronicus' offer of peace. Peace was all the more necessary in view of the threat to his northern frontiers from the Hungarians. Under the terms of peace Dushan retained Ohrid, Prilep (which became the Serbian capital) and some other towns.

Dushan then turned to meet the threat from Hungary. Charles of Hungary, however, in view of the inadequate forces at his disposal, decided to avoid an open conflict with the Serbians and withdrew his army from the Danube. According to Danilo the withdrawal was carried out in great disorder. Cantacuzene's assertion that Andronicus provided help to Dushan against Hungary cannot be accepted in view of the danger to the Empire from the Turks in Asia Minor, which was one of the reasons why the Emperor had made peace with Dushan in the first place. The fact that Andronicus had arrived at Salonika with only a small force implied that he was short of troops, and it was in the interests of the Empire that Dushan should be involved in a war with Hungary which would keep him too occupied to threaten the Empire. His immediate object in making peace with Dushan had been to secure his rear, leaving him free to advance into Thessaly and Epirus.

Military action against Hungary seems to have been discontinued, for in 1335 Dushan was once again active in Macedonia. Andronicus had returned to Salonika hoping once more to bring Thessaly and Albania under his control, and raising doubts in the mind of Dushan about the value of the peace he had concluded with the Emperor. The struggle with the Latins and the Turks called Andronicus back to the east, and in order to secure the west from a new Serbian attack he had recourse to diplomacy. During his attack on Phocus and Lesbos, Dushan refrained from advancing into Macedonia and, as if he were co-operating with the Emperor, he attacked the Latin possessions on the eastern coast of the Adriatic. In 1336 he advanced to central Albania, concentrating above all on the city of Drac which recognised the rule of the Angevins. Having devastated the surrounding countryside he entered into negotiations with the boyars who surrendered the town to him. He refrained, however, from invading the territories of the Angevin rulers.

Technically Dushan was at peace with the Empire; the attempt by Andronicus to re-establish his control in Albania provided Dushan with a pretext for a renewal of hostilities against the Empire. When Andronicus advanced to Epirus, Dushan seized important points in central Albania, and by 1337 the towns of Avlon and Kanin were in Serbian hands. Taking advantage of the difficulties Andronicus was encountering in his efforts to subdue Epirus, Dushan advanced gradually to the south, and by 1340 the whole of the formerly independent Albania was in his hands and he assumed the title King of Albania, encountering no resistance from Byzantium. The Albanians, though not without a struggle, recognised Serbian rule. Representatives of the Albanian boyars entered into negotiations with the Angevins in which they expressed their willingness to help in the recovery of the kingdom and its restoration to Angevin rule. A Serbian army invaded Albania and was defeated by an Albanian boyar named Andrew Musak, who was rewarded with the title of Despot of Epirus. The victory had no long term results; the Albanians received no help from Byzantium and were forced to come to terms with Dushan. Dushan had acquired an important wedge of territory between the Despotate of Epirus and Thessaly (the dukedom of Vlach) and was strategically well placed to mount an attack against either state. He did not continue his advance in that area, however, but turned once more to Macedonia where the situation offered greater possibilities of easy victories.

On the death of Andronicus III which was followed by a power struggle between the Empress Anna and her son against Cantacuzene, Serbian troops entered Macedonia and advanced on Salonika, meeting no resistance from the Byzantine army. The Serbians contented themselves with grabbing as much as they could and returned to their sovereign. Cantacuzene, now virtual ruler of the Byzantine Empire, drew up a plan of campaign in the Peloponnese, but considered it politically advisable to maintain friendly relations with Dushan and sent ambassadors for the purpose of renewing the negotiations entered into between Dushan and the late Emperor. Peace, however, did not last for long; the critical situation developing in the Empire as a result of the civil war, soon to break out between Cantacuzene and the Emperor John Palaeologus, was too tempting for Dushan to remain detached, or to link himself permanently to one side or the other. The ideal situation from his point of view would be to see the civil war prolonged, and if he did intervene, this intervention should be decided by the interests of Serbia.

Cantacuzene was the first to turn to Dushan for help. When he appeared in the western provinces to seek help in regaining Constantinople, he found Macedonia in a critical state. In the south Salonika and Serres were under the rule of Byzantine regents; the whole of the north was controlled by Dushan, while Serbian influence was decisive in those areas not under direct Serbian control. One part of Macedonia was ruled by Chrel, a vassal of Dushan, who now declared himself independent. Although his principality was small it was strategically important. Cantacuzene had already established contact with many of the Serbian nobles and turned in particular to Chrel with whom he had a meeting. Shortly afterwards Chrel was admitted to the monastery of Ril, and in 1343 the Serbian army occupied Strumnits and Melnik which had been previously ruled by him. Dushan meanwhile, as if ignoring the military diversions of Cantacuzene and Chrel, was besieging Edessa but was forced to withdraw to avoid an open conflict with the approaching Byzantine army in view of the technical state of peace existing between Serbia and the Empire.

As a preliminary to the formation of an alliance with Dushan, Cantacuzene despatched an ambassador to the King to seek support. Then at the head of a small force he advanced into Serbian territory where he was welcomed by a Serbian noble near Prosek. Cantacuzene was aware of the power and influence of the Serbian nobles and no doubt believed that if he could win them to his side they would put pressure on the King. One of the most powerful of these nobles was Oliver, to whom Cantacuzene turned for support, offering his son Manuel as husband to Oliver's daughter. Oliver, who was favourably disposed to Cantacuzene – no doubt for his own ends – contacted Dushan, who was preparing with his wife Helen to visit Bulgaria. It is doubtful whether Oliver was able to persuade the King of the necessity of a meeting with Cantacuzene; nevertheless the news that the pretender to the imperial throne was in Serbian territory was enough to make him postpone his Bulgarian journey and a meeting took place near Pristrin with the usual honours. But this did not alter the fact that Cantacuzene came as a suppliant, utterly dependent on Serbian help; he recalled the ancient friendship which had existed between him and Dushan but was not prepared in his own words to give up 'one iota of the Empire'.

The question of agreement with Cantacuzene was not one that could be decided by the King alone, but depended on the nobles and the Queen whose brother Oliver appeared to support Cantacuzene's claim to the Empire. In fact the nobles were keener than the King to interfere in the civil war; war offered the prospects of territory. (When on an earlier occasion Milutin agreed to make peace with Byzantium he was bitterly criticised by the nobles.) Dushan dreamed of obtaining Southern Macedonia, Boetia, Thessaly and Epirus. These conditions were quite unacceptable to Cantacuzene; a willingness on his part to renounce large parts of the Empire was bound to strengthen the position of his enemies in Constantinople.

He delivered a lecture to the King on the true value of friendship, and announced his intention of seeking other means of support which did not involve the break-up of the Empire. In fact this was bluff; if he failed to obtain help from Dushan there was no-one else to turn to. Moreover there was always the possibility that Dushan might be persuaded to join John Palaeologus. Cantacuzene, according to his own account, then promised, once the Empire had been secured, to support Dushan against his enemies; in return Dushan promised military help, openly acknowledging Cantacuzene's rights as Emperor, and renouncing any claims to Byzantine territory. This evidence must be treated with caution; Cantacuzene here 'departs somewhat from the truth'. It is impossible to believe that Dushan should have been prepared to commit his forces to a war from which no territorial advantages were to be gained. Gregoras, who had no reason to lie, states that the future of territories captured by the Serbians would be settled by negotiation. Thus Dushan was acting in the interests of Serbia; he was not committed to Cantacuzene in principle, and in the civil war within the Empire both sides turned to him for support. The opportunity for quick and easy gains was too good to miss.

Operations began with an attack by Cantacuzene at the head of a Serbian army and his own small force against the city of Serres, but the attempt to capture it failed, partly due to the fierce resistance of the citizens who remained loyal to the Emperor, partly to the effects of disease among the troops. The failure to capture Serres and the heavy losses suffered by his troops weakened Dushan's resolve to continue support for Cantacuzene. The refusal of the city to submit to the latter opened up the prospect of the city falling to Dushan himself. Failing this he could compensate himself by gaining territory elsewhere; forestalling Cantacuzene, he laid siege to Edessa which by means of negotiations and bribery soon fell into his hands. Meanwhile Cantacuzene, forced to leave Serbia, advanced into southern Macedonia, evidently with the intention of taking Edessa; finding it occupied by Serbian garrisons he was forced to reconcile himself to its loss. It was evident to him that Dushan was pursuing his own aims. Independently of the failure to take Serres – which remained an ultimate objective – no further advantage was to be gained by Dushan continuing to support Cantacuzene, particularly when the latter's opponents were making overtures to him.

While the siege of Serres was under way ambassadors from Constantinople arrived in Serbia. In the name of the Emperor they asked Dushan to hand over Cantacuzene, promising in return some territories which the King might choose. Dushan was not in a position to accept this offer; a considerable part of his troops was under the control of Cantacuzene, and to come to an agreement with Constantinople would be improper and dangerous. Dushan was then offered all Macedonia up to Christopol, excluding Salonika, provided he withdrew his support from Cantacuzene and kept him under watch. Cantacuzene found support at the Serbian court, in particular from the Queen and some of the nobles; he claimed that one Serbian noble who expressed support for the Emperor was threatened with death. It is fairly certain that if Dushan was not prepared openly to support the party of the Emperor it had nothing to do with Cantacuzene and everything to do with the interests of Serbia.

Nothing, perhaps, indicates more clearly the real attitude of Dushan towards his ally than the attack on Serres which Cantacuzene attempted with the help of Serbian troops finally to subdue. This time success was even less likely than before. The forces at his disposal were too weak for the task; more important, Dushan was not willing to see Cantacuzene gain control of this vital strategic point. If Dushan himself was not to gain control it was preferable that it should remain in the hands of the Emperor. Cantacuzene hoped no doubt that the rulers of the city would be prepared to hand it over to him, something which Dushan was determined to prevent. In fact Constantin Palaeologus, the governor of the city and the Metropolitan were bitter enemies of Cantacuzene, but equally they refused to hand it over to Dushan. But if Serres remained unconquered, Serbian gains at the expense of Cantacuzene outweighed any benefits which the latter had gained from his alliance with Dushan. In the course of seven months Serbia had gained a significant increase in territory at the expense of the Empire; Dushan was winning an empire not for Cantacuzene but for himself, and every success for Dushan was a defeat for his ally. Clearly Cantacuzene was now a hindrance to him and more might be gained by joining the other side which was potentially more dangerous than Cantacuzene. The latter was aware that he could expect no more help from Dushan. On the contrary, his main worry was that the latter would seize the greater part of Macedonia and would be prepared to hand him over to his enemies.

His position in Serbia remained difficult; his failure on both occasions to capture Serres weakened his influence. The majority of those who were influential in Serbian affairs, and who had provided his main support in the past, were now hostile. The Serbian nobles who expected material rewards from the war were unlikely to back a loser. Only the Queen as before continued to give him her support. The war had drained his resources, much of these going on lavish presents to the Serbian nobles and the payment to Serbian units under his control. Nothing could be gained by his further co-operation with Dushan and he decided to act independently. His main objective at this point was Verri, an important city in Boetia, which he was able to take partly by guile and partly because one party in the city supported him. This gave him a safe sanctuary and a powerful point of resistance for further military activity. Most of the towns in Boetia hastened to recognise his rule. The support which he now enjoyed in Thessaly put him in a position to advance on Salonika probably in the spring of 1348.

This change in the fortunes of Cantacuzene was a blow to Dushan. The unexpected conquest of a province which he himself had prepared to attack convinced him that the time had come to declare open war against his former ally. But for some time he did nothing, hoping perhaps to achieve his aims by agreement with the party of the Emperor. He demanded the return of the Latin-German units he had provided for the use of Cantacuzene, but these refused to abandon their leader. Dushan then turned to the leaders in Salonika and proposed joint action against the common enemy. However a much greater danger faced Cantacuzene; on hearing that a powerful imperial army had landed in Salonika, he abandoned his plans to attack the city and returned to Verri. A Serbian army attacked him as he crossed the Vardar.

Cantacuzene later claimed that Dushan attempted to conceal his part in the affair, disclaiming all responsibility on the grounds that the army had acted without his knowledge. It may be that Dushan hesitated openly to act against his former ally until and unless he could obtain a guarantee of compensation for joining the Emperor. Apokav from Constantinople tried to bribe the King and tried to persuade the Queen and the nobles to put pressure on him to support the Emperor. His efforts seem to have failed, and attempts were made to involve Venice as intermediary. The Venetian Senate stated that in view of the plea of the Empress Anna and her son an embassy should be sent to the Serbian king in an effort to establish friendly relations between him and the Emperor. The main object of the embassy of course was to ensure the interests of the Republic but it seems to have had some success. Dushan suggested a meeting with Cantacuzene with the object of capturing him and handing him over to his enemies. The plot failed; Cantacuzene, advised by his friends, rejected the proposal and sent instead his son Manuel. Dushan thereupon declared negotiations at an end, and combined a declaration of war with support for the Emperor.

Dushan's agreement with the Emperor was of a more negative character than his alliance with Cantacuzene had been. The policy of the imperial party was rather to deprive Cantacuzene of Serbian support, and they would be satisfied with a policy of neutrality from Dushan. On the other hand, while breaking with Cantacuzene, Dushan did not openly proclaim his adherence to the Emperor. He attempted to recover the lost territories of Boetia, but acted on his own and not on the Emperor's behalf, nor were his attacks confined only to towns supporting Cantacuzene. The longer the civil war continued the easier it would be for him to gain Byzantine territory. A military alliance with the Emperor had certain advantages in that it would paralyse all attempts from that quarter to frustrate his military plans. By the summer of 1343 he was openly proclaiming his support for the Emperor; there is no evidence that he undertook any military activity in the second half of the year. Southern Macedonia was then overrun by various Turkish hordes. 'Historians usually call Cantacuzene the sole cause of the first establishment of the Turks in the Balkans; he called on them for help during the struggle with John Palaeologus.' These troops were likely to act independently when the opportunity offered. In fact both sides used Turkish mercenaries. Under the leadership of Avakov they devastated Boetia while they awaited Serbian troops for a combined attack against Cantacuzene. A Turkish army under Cantacuzene forced Avakov to withdraw, invaded Macedonia and attacked areas held by the Serbians.

There is no evidence of Dushan taking steps to repel the Turkish invasion; it may be he was unwilling to risk a confrontation with such a powerful army – possibly he lacked the strength. Only at the end of the following year did he appear at the head of an army in Macedonia which in the following three years became the main battleground. The province was falling into a state of chaos. Salonika refused to recognise either Cantacuzene or John Palaeologus and was controlled by the anarchic-democratic party of the Zealots. Manuel Cantacuzene still held Verri for his father, but Serres and some lesser towns remained loyal to the Emperor. The situation in Macedonia, weak and helpless before the assault of Serbians and Turks, was desperate. Nevertheless it took Dushan some six months to establish his control and he failed to capture Salonika. This suggests that there were obstacles in the path of an easy victory; the cities were generally hostile and the military forces at his disposal were limited, and in the case of siege warfare ineffective. The main part of the army consisted of German and Italian mercenaries provided by Venice. They were well armed but of little use before a fortified town; the ability of these latter to resist a siege is seen time and again, the classic example being Salonika which never fell. The bulk of the Serbian troops were involved in operations elsewhere. Finally the Serbians were weakened as a result of the defeat they suffered at the hands of the Turks in 1344; no-one yet realised that the real victor in all these wars were the Turks.

It is not possible to chart the course of events in the years 1344-45 in Macedonia. From time to time mention is made of the King conquering more and more towns but these are not named. Once Dushan had established control in Macedonia he turned to the south-east where the rich and powerful city of Serres remained unconquered. However, for reasons which are not clear he bypassed the city and advanced to Zihn. Cantacuzene asserts that he was preparing an attack from the rear in Thrace; in fact Dushan did not advance beyond Macedonia. His strategy was to reduce the towns, after which he seized Zihn. To conquer all this territory and Christopol and undertake the siege of Serres was beyond his powers, because of the need to protect his northern borders against the Hungarians.

Alarmed at the defeat he had suffered at the hands of Cantacuzene's Turkish allies at the Battle of Stefiano, he abandoned Zihn and retreated to his own territories. As a result the Turks were able without resistance to advance across Macedonia and join with Cantacuzene.

The Serbian defeat temporarily ended further military activity in Macedonia by Dushan. Returning to his capital – Skopje or Strumnits – he, in the words of Cantacuzene 'did not sleep but continued the war'. Units of Serbian troops were despatched for the defence of the hinterland of Salonika and Boetia but as always Salonika, 'a Greek island in a Slav sea' remained impregnable. The Serbian hold was strengthened in the area between Verri and Christopol. The population of this area, a mixture of Bulgarians, Greeks and Albanians, submitted to Serbian rule, if only because they saw in Dushan the most effective, perhaps the only defence against the Turks who were extending their domination over an increasing part of Macedonia. In the towns there were pro-Serbian elements among the citizens who saw in Dushan the only safeguard against anarchy. Manuel Cantacuzene, ruling in the name of his father and deprived of support, was finally restricted to the city of Verri, and was forced under pressure from the pro-Serbian faction to leave the city. His flight was followed by the capture of the city by Serbian troops probably in 1345. But Serres remained the prime objective of Dushan. He recognised the strategic importance of the city lying between the eastern and western parts of the Empire, control of which would ensure the territories of Macedonia from the east. He lacked the strength however to take the city by storm, and resorted to the customary means of subduing fortified cities – siege and starvation. From time to time the siege was lifted to relieve and provision the army, as well as to avoid conflict with the Turkish mercenaries of Cantacuzene for whom, after the defeat of Stefiano he had a healthy respect. After the first assault the rulers of Serres, seeing no prospect of relief from Cantacuzene, negotiated terms of surrender. Cantacuzene was too involved in Thrace to undertake a diversion in Macedonia. By the summer of 1345, having for the moment defeated his enemies, and established his control over the greater part of Thrace, he was prepared with the support of his Turkish allies to save the city from the Serbians, but the attempt failed.

The siege was renewed; the situation inside the city was desperate. A strong pro-Serbian faction headed by Irene Cantacuzene demanded a voluntary surrender to Dushan. Cantacuzene, informed of the danger threatening Serres, directed his armies to Christopol. News of the approaching Turks again forced Dushan to withdraw from the city. But Cantacuzene failed to appear; he was defeated by a Turkish army in the pay of the Emperor, and returned to Constantinople where a rising had taken place. The exact date of the surrender of the city is not known, but by

October 1345 the city was certainly in the hands of Dushan. This is clear from a charter of October of that year, in answer to a request from the monks of Menoikeion to the King as ruler of Serres. Two other documents, one to Venice, the other to Dubrovnik, were written in Serres.

The fall of Serres sealed the fate of Macedonia; along with Albania it became part of the Serbian Empire. Only Salonika defied all efforts to conquer it. Over a period of 15 years Dushan had almost doubled his territories at the expense of the Byzantine Empire. These conquests had been achieved with comparatively little effort, but there was an element of luck in all this. The war within the Empire, the Turkish threat in Asia Minor, the defenceless state of the provinces, the lack of solidarity among a population composed of different races and nationalities, all contributed to his success. Only in Albania was there any organised resistance; there the Serbians had to employ considerable forces in that area, the mountainous nature of which remained the main obstacle to successful military action. Macedonia, on the other hand, was completely at his mercy. The towns which as we have seen always proved difficult to win, fell to him largely as a result of the passivity of the inhabitants, or as in the case of Serres, as a result of a 'fifth column' of pro-Serbians. The main danger came not from the Empire but from the Turks who delayed the final conquest of Macedonia. Finally we must always remember the limited forces at the disposal of Dushan; he preferred to achieve his aims by negotiations rather than by war.

The capture of Serres which set the seal on his Macedonian conquests was soon followed by his assumption of the imperial title. As a ruler of vast territories won from the Empire 'there was nothing to stop him extending his powers and supreme rule over the other Greek lands up to Byzantium itself and proclaiming himself Emperor of the Romans – and triumphantly assuming the tiara and the purple'. These words of Gregoras are echoed by Cantacuzene. 'The King conquered Serres – after that, seeing himself ruler of the greater part of the Empire, he proclaimed himself Emperor of the Romans and the Serbians, granting his son the title of King.' In western Macedonia the population included Bulgarians, Vlachs and Albanians. Only Salonika could be regarded as purely Greek. The situation in eastern Macedonia was different; here the Greeks predominated. As a ruler of these lands Dushan could claim, not without justification, to be ruler not only of Bulgarians and Vlachs but also of Greeks. In a letter to the Doge of Venice he describes himself as 'King of Serbia, Dioclea, Hum, Zeta, Albania and Pomorski (Littoral), ruler of a large part of the Bulgarian Empire and master of almost all of the Byzantine Empire'. Logically the next step was to be crowned as Emperor, not only of the Serbians, since his empire consisted of many different races, but Emperor of the 'Romans'. He was not, of course, the first Slav ruler to have dreamed of founding a new Slav Empire to replace Byzantium.

If he was not acquainted with the history of Simeon of Bulgaria, he was certainly aware of the achievements of Asen, the founder of the Second Bulgarian Empire and his powerful successor Asenil. His residence in areas in which the traditions of the Bulgarian Empire had survived may have strengthened his resolve to create his own empire. It must have been humiliating to remain simply as King when his neighbours, less powerful than himself such as John Alexander of Bulgaria, bore the title of Emperor. But Dushan's ambitions extended beyond the mere creation of a Serbian rival empire to that of Byzantium; the Serbian kingdom and the Slav lands united with it should be only part of the 'Roman' Empire with Dushan replacing the Palaeologi and himself ruling in Constantinople. Hence the importance of the coronation of his son Urosh as King and ruler of the Serbian lands, while the newly conquered Greek lands remained in his own hands, thus following the example of the Byzantine emperors.

Although Dushan proclaimed himself Emperor in January 1346, the actual ceremony was carried out in the following April in Skopje. But it is possible that a previous coronation had taken place in Serres soon after the capture of the city. In the winter of the year 1345 a Serbian council (sabor) assembled at Serres with the object of proclaiming Dushan as Emperor of the Serbians and Greeks (tsar Sr'blem i Grkom) 'imperator Rascie et Romani'. The title of King was given to Urosh who was still a minor. An ambassador was sent to Venice to inform the Senate of the preparations for the coronation and to offer an alliance against the Emperor. The Senate sent its congratulations but rejected the proposed alliance on the grounds of Venetian involvement with Hungary and the negotiations they were conducting with the Emperor. In accordance with Byzantine custom the coronation of the Emperor required the imperial robe and crown and the triumphal proclamation. Moreover the laws of the Orthodox Church demanded that the Emperor be crowned by the Patriarch. The Serbian archbishop was raised to the rank of Patriarch and was supported by the Patriarch of Bulgaria in Trnovo and the Archbishop of Ohrid.

From the coronation at Serres to the triumphant crowning at Skopje was a period of about six months, during which time Dushan was almost entirely involved in new attacks against the lands of the Emperor. But his aim, now that he had conquered non-Serbian territory, was to reconcile the subject peoples, Greek aristocrats and Church leaders, and gradually to prepare himself for his role as Byzantine Emperor. One result of this was the introduction of Byzantine customs and titles which were a marked feature of his court. Regarding himself as Emperor of the Greeks in the territories from the Vardar to Christopol, he resolved to rule these according to

Byzantine custom. All civic duties and government of the territories were allotted for the most part to Greeks, probably those who had held them prior to the conquest. In Serres the first *kefali* after the conquest was a Greek whose name is referred to in a charter of 1346, 'after the creation of my empire (dvoranin tsarva mi) George Fokopulo obtained the position of kefali – of Serres'. A charter of 1349 refers to Manuel Liver, Voivod of Valero, Serres and Strum. Greeks entrusted with government posts bore the title of *domestos:* Alexis Raul, Andronicus Cantacuzene among others. It is probable that some of them bore the titles from the Byzantine court and continued to bear them under the new order. In the case of Andronicus the title was a reward for his services to Dushan. To what extent the titles and duties involved in the newly established Serbo-Greek court coincided with those existing at the Byzantine court is difficult to determine. Given the fact that these were men of experience and the Serbians were not, it is likely that the conquest made little difference to their position. Greek was the official language along with Serbian; in this way Dushan counted on attracting to himself the Greek autocrats in the conquered territories.

Equally important was the support of the Greek clergy. The episcopal sees and holy places, not only in the Greek part of Macedonia, but also in the Slav lands and even in Serbia itself, were held for the most part by Greeks. Co-operation and support from the Greek clergy could be a source of strength, countering the power of the unruly nobles. In accordance with the traditions of the Empire, Dushan was aware that the proclamation as Emperor would be legally invalid without the sanctification of the highest spiritual authority. The Archbishop of Serbia, subordinate to the Patriarch of Constantinople, could not exercise this authority. A Serbian archbishop had the right only to sanctify Dushan as Serbian Emperor; for the sanctification as Emperor of the Greeks something more was required. No support for an independent Church could be expected from Constantinople. Above all, recognition from and support for the independent Church in Serbia from the clergy and fathers of Mount Athos was essential, since the Holy Mountain exercised great influence over the Orthodox world. It is no reflection on the piety of Dushan to suggest that the lavish gifts to the monasteries had a political motive.

One example of his generosity to the Church is connected with the monastery of St. John the Baptist near Serres. After Athens one of the most important religious centres of the Empire, it was now under Serbian rule. Immediately after the capture of Serres, Dushan issued a charter to the monastery in which he guaranteed the immunity of the monastic property, not only confirming all previous rights granted by Byzantium, but granting the estates of Lascar belonging to Cantacuzene, along with mills, parks and villages. In a charter of 1348 he granted lands to the church of the

Archangels Michael and Gabriel near Prizren, of whom the first *igumen* was the Serbian Metropolitan Jacob.

There were underlying reasons for Dushan's actions so far as the Church was concerned. At the beginning of 1346 he granted a charter to some of the monasteries of Mount Athos. During the 14th century the greater part of the monasteries including Serbian and Bulgarian belonged to the Greeks, and from 1315 were subject to the Patriarch of Constantinople. In addition the Byzantine Emperor established his protection over all of Mount Athos. Serbian and Bulgarian rulers had no control over their monasteries; the situation was clearly understood and accepted. The Emperor was ruler of the territory which included Mount Athos and Macedonia. Now the order of things had changed; after the capture of Serres by the Serbians, Macedonia ceased to belong to the Emperor. A new Emperor of the 'Romans' had appeared in whose hands lay the fate of Mount Athos. Sometime towards the beginning of 1346 Dushan visited the Holy Mountain. No attempt was made by the Serbian army to penetrate Athos itself, probably because of the religious awe it exerted on the peoples of the Orthodox world. Nevertheless the fathers of the Greek monasteries could not fail to be aware that the protection of their lands had been transferred from Byzantium to the Serbian Emperor, on whom they must rely for future favours. Dushan calmed their fears and doubts. Not only did he confirm all existing rights but made new grants and accepted all the obligations as protector of Mount Athos, thereby obliging the monks to recognise him as Emperor of the 'Romans'. The recognition of the imperial title by what was, in effect, the spiritual centre of the 'Byzantine Commonwealth' would sanctify him and legalise his actions. After the capture of Serres he not only granted gifts to the Serbian monastery of Hilander but also to the Greek monasteries.

In April 1346 the second coronation of Dushan took place at Skopje. Among those in attendance were leading figures from the Serbian kingdom, the Serbian clergy headed by the Archbishop John, the Patriarch of Trnovo and the Bulgarian bishops, Greek clergy from the conquered territories, the Archbishop of Ohrid and fathers from Mount Athos. They were there to sanctify a new empire. The first day's business was taken up with the establishment of the new Serbian Patriarchate. Having established his complete independence from the Empire of Byzantium in the military and political field, it was natural that Dushan should wish to have a Church completely independent of Constantinople. 'The Empire without a Patriarch was unthinkable.' He could point to the example of Bulgaria, where the assumption of the imperial title had been followed by the creation of an independent Bulgarian Church with a Patriarch at its head. Indeed at that time his fellow Bulgarian ruler had his Patriarch at Trnovo. But above all the Patriarch was needed for the coronation. The head of the Serbian Church must be the main figure in the coronation ceremony, and it was necessary that he should be on an equal footing with the Patriarch of Trnovo; from the concept of the Empire as the highest form of government it followed that the Emperor must be invested by the supreme spiritual power, and this in the Orthodox Church belonged to the Patriarch.

The circumstances under which the Serbian Patriarchate was established differed from those prevailing on the occasion of the establishment of the Patriarchate of Bulgaria, which had been approved by a Council of Greek and Bulgarian clergy and confirmed by the Patriarch of Constantinople and the Patriarchs of the East. In Serbia, however, the Patriarchate was established, not by law nor the approval of the Patriarch of Constantinople to which the Church of Serbia was subordinate, but by a Serbian Council. Did Dushan consult Constantinople over the question of the Patriarchate or did he decide to do without the agreement of legal authority? He would certainly want to ensure that his imperial title was recognised as legally valid, which in the eyes of the Greeks would only be the case if the Patriarch of Serbia had been recognised by Constantinople. From one point of view the approval of Constantinople was unnecessary; Dushan had the military power, large areas of Byzantine territories were in his hands. But it is an indication of the influence, the mystique of Byzantium, even in decline, on the minds of the Slav rulers who opposed it, that they should have felt the need to imitate its customs. That Dushan's coronation should be carried out within the strict letter of the law as defined by Byzantium was in any case essential if he were seriously to lay claim to the imperial crown. The situation in the Empire was one calculated to favour Dushan. In the event he was not prepared to wait for long; for him it was necessary to sanctify his title as soon as possible. A request for approval to establish a Serbian Patriarchate would almost certainly have met with a refusal from Constantinople. The government of the Empress Anna and the Patriarch, living through the last days of their rule, had little time to deal with external affairs. Nothing was to be gained by a policy of appeasement towards Dushan. Thus the Serbian Patriarchate was established without the presence or the approval of the Patriarch of Constantinople. Dushan himself appointed Joannik as Patriarch. The assembled clergy, the Serbian bishops, the Patriarch of Bulgaria and the Archbishop of Ohrid simply accepted the fait accompli. The Patriarch of Constantinople refused to recognise the legality and Serbia lay under the ban of excommunication from 1352-1375.

The establishment of the Patriarchate was followed by the triumphant coronation of Dushan as Emperor. The *igumen* and fathers of Mount Athos and the 'Archbishop of the Greek capital' had to confirm Dushan's assumption of the imperial title as Emperor not only of the Serbians but of the Greeks. But the name of Serbia still took pride of place in all the writings and charters of Dushan; until the final and complete conquest of all the lands of the Empire he could not consider himself as Emperor of the 'Romans'. This remained the object of his ambitions but he was not at that time in a position to realise it, and he was still only Emperor of the Serbians and his main strength lay in the lands he had inherited. In addition Dushan considered himself as liberator of the other Slav peoples (rodnago naroda) from the hegemony of the Emperor in Constantinople. In the ceremony of the crowning were included the words 'Emperor of the Bulgarians and Albanians (tsar Bolgarom i Arbanosom)' which can also be found in his charters. This would imply the inclusion of Albania within his empire and is the first mention of his rule over Bulgarians as an ethnic component of his conquered territories, i.e. Bulgarians living outside the Bulgarian state and former subjects of the Byzantine Empire. But it may also be seen as expressing a claim to the Bulgarian throne.

In accordance with Byzantine custom Dushan's wife Helen was also crowned as Empress, while his son, the 10-year-old Urosh was crowned as 'King of the Serbian lands'. The Empress and her son were now associated with the government and their names appear along with that of Dushan on all important acts. For Urosh at this age there could be no question of his governing the 'Serbian lands' but the decision of the Emperor to have him crowned as King of all the Serbian lands confirms his intention of regarding these lands as a special part of the monarchy.

Apart from the leading representatives of the Church some of the Slav rulers of the Balkans were present at the coronation. From Bulgaria came not only the Patriarch and clergy but also members of the Bulgarian royal family. Ambassadors from Dubrovnik attended the coronation; their names have been recorded. In the name of the Republic they greeted the newly crowned Emperor and presented him with gifts. Similar letters of congratulation were received from Venice. The new court was first established at Serres. The coronation was followed by the distribution of honours and titles to those deemed worthy, for services rendered. The Emperor's brother-in-law Oliver was given the title of Despot, another member of the royal family was made sebastocrat; other names included that of Vukashin, created Despot, and his brother Uglesh 'comes stabularius'. To mark the occasion of the coronation Dushan instituted the military order of St. Stephen; one of the first recipients was the ambassador from Dubrovnik who had attended the coronation.

The presence of the Bulgarian Patriarch along with other members of the Church at the coronation ceremony implied the sanction of the Church for the changes carried out by Dushan in the Balkans. But ultimate sanction lay with the leaders of the Greek clergy, i.e. the Patriarch of Constantinople and the fathers of Mount Athos. From the former as we have seen no support could be expected. Dushan, therefore, concentrated his attention on Mount Athos; he had already, prior to his coronation, tried to win them over to his side. He was ready to express his gratitude in tangible form. He confirmed the independence of the archbishopric of Ohrid which it had enjoyed prior to the conquest of Macedonia. In a charter dated May 1346 to the monastery of Vatoped, the Emperor 'taking over the care and defence formerly exercised by St. Simeon (Nemanje) and Sava' confirms the proprietorial rights of the monastery and grants the village of Mamantos, frees the monastery and the villages belonging to it from the payment of taxes, and returns lands which have been lost. In the following year, 1347, Dushan in the company of his wife and the leading clergy paid a visit to Athos, spending some four months visiting all the monasteries, and receiving the thanks of the fathers. Seven charters issued by Dushan are connected with the visit – no doubt there were more. Four charters refer to the monastery of Hilander; after the conquest of Macedonia and the peninsula of Athos, Dushan stood as direct protector of the Serbian monastery. By his generosity to Athos he was staking a claim to be regarded as the new imperial ruler of the Orthodox world.

CHAPTER III

Dushan and Constantinople
Relations with Venice
Relations with Bulgaria
Relations with Hungary and the Papacy

Relations with Venice

THE CROWNING OF DUSHAN was not the final act in the drama but rather the prelude to a new attack on the Empire. The coronation was merely the open expression of his secret ambitions, which he attempted to realise in the course of the second half of his reign. Later successes were not so easily achieved as those which had culminated in the conquest of Macedonia; partly this was due to the fact that his attentions were sometimes directed elsewhere: the war with Bosnia, the Hungarian attack and resistance within his own territories. Those diversions delayed but did not lead him to renounce his ambitions, which aimed at nothing less than the conquest of the entire Byzantine Empire and his establishment as Emperor at Constantinople. Gregoras attributes to Dushan the belief that with the capture of Serres he would meet with no resistance in subjecting the Empire and Constantinople itself. If this view is correct, and there is no evidence that Dushan ever openly expressed such ambitions, it was a reasonable deduction following the assumption of the imperial title. The comparative ease with which he conquered the south-east was a consequence of Byzantine weakness.

Dushan had spent his youth in exile with his father in Constantinople and was well informed about the strategic position of the capital and the impossibility of capturing it by siege; open to the sea, the city could not be starved into submission like the cities of Macedonia. It was clear that the first necessity was a fleet which Dushan did not possess. For this reason he turned to Venice, the greatest naval power in the Adriatic. He believed that by granting concessions to the Venetians he could win their support and capture Constantinople. But although Venice shared with Dushan a common hostility to the Empire, the Venetians were not prepared to see the Palaeologi replaced by a Serbian emperor. A study of the policies of Venice towards the Empire clearly showed Venetian aims to be incompatible with the ambitions of Dushan. Taking an active part in the conquest of Constantinople – for which they were richly rewarded – the Venetians retained control of Crete and other islands after the reconquest in 1261. In fact their power and influence were much greater and they were effective masters of the Greek archipelago, controlling all trade between Greece and the islands, Syria and Egypt on the one hand, and masters of the west on the other. Their determination to see Constantinople once more under Western control was equally as strong as the determination of Dushan to capture it. Apart from that it was difficult for the Venetians to reconcile themselves to the fact that some territories of the Empire were controlled by their inveterate enemies the Genoese.

Venice, therefore, had two aims; to see the restoration of the 'Latin' Empire, and to destroy the power of the Genoese. Venetian ambitions of establishing the power of Venice on the shores of the Bosphorus are clearly expressed in the titles which the Doge adopted 'as rulers of one fourth and one eighth of the Empire of the Romans'. Obviously then if the Venetians captured Constantinople it would be for themselves. But at the same time the Republic lacked the military strength for an attack against the Empire; they found it impossible to undertake military action against the powerful Genoese who, controlling Galatea, stoutly defended the unfortunate capital from attack by the Venetian rival. If, therefore, an alliance with the West was desirable from Dushan's point of view, Genoa seemed preferable to Venice.

The Western powers, hoping to overthrow the Empire, were not likely willingly to accept the creation of another Orthodox empire – and one which seemed more capable of defending itself. Dushan failed to understand this; obsessed with the idea of capturing Constantinople, he seriously believed that Venice would be prepared to co-operate in this undertaking. In any case the long term aims of Venice in the Adriatic conflicted with those of Dushan; these were to strengthen their power by asserting their control of Dalmatia and the Serbo-Croat Littoral, an aim going back to the 10th or 11th century, from which period the Doge bore the title Duke of Dalmatia, indicating long term aims rather than present reality. After a series of unsuccessful attempts and continual fighting with Neretians, Croats, Byzantines, Normans and Hungarians, by the 14th century they had virtually achieved their aims. All important political and trading centres from Istria to Dubrovnik, nearly all the islands within that area were to a greater or lesser extent dependent on Venice. Zadar, Skradin, Trogir, Split, Dubrovnik, the islands of Krc, Osor, Rab, all recognised the government of the Venetian state, were governed by Venetian counts, paid taxes to Venice and recognised military obligations to the Republic. The Venetians were the closest neighbours of Dushan. If an alliance with Dushan against Byzantium was unacceptable because it offered no advantages to Venice, there were other inducements which might alter the Venetian attitude. While it is true that the Venetian fleet dominated the Adriatic, the commercial links with the Slav hinterland were relatively weak. Almost all the trade in the western part of the Balkan peninsula was in the hands of Dubrovnik which, though dependent on Venice, still maintained long standing trading privileges in the Slav lands. Generally speaking the influence of Venice was confined to the Littoral and did not extend far inland. The Venetians aim was to gather all the trade of the peninsula into their hands. This was a factor which could force Venice into alliance with Dushan; it offered an opportunity to extend their commercial influence in the Balkans. Another factor influencing Serbo-Venetian relations arose from the hostility which existed towards Venice; the Dalmatian Council for instance was always ready to renounce Venetian control. A greater threat, however, came from Hungary where the King laid claim to Dalmatia and the lands of the south-west Balkans. In the face of such threats an alliance with Dushan offered definite advantages. The Republic was willing to enter into friendly relations with Dushan, endeavouring on the one hand to gain as much advantage as they could, while on the other trying to ensure that his aims were restricted so far as his plans for an attack against Constantinople were concerned, making it clear to him that his aims were incompatible with the interests of Venice.

The earliest records of commercial relations between Venice and the Serbian crown date from the second half of the 13th century, and deal with a request from the Great Council for an inquiry into the arrest in Serbia of Venetian citizens. It is reasonable to assume that commercial links between the two states existed long before this date. One of the trade routes by which caravans plied between Byzantium and the provinces on the one hand, and the Adriatic on the other, passed through Serbian territory. A Venetian M.S. dating from the 14th century includes among the names of the Slav leaders that of 'Urosius, rex Servie' clearly referring to Urosh the Great (1243). Trading links therefore existed between Serbia and Venice in the first half of the 13th century, but these links were insignificant. Venetian control over Dalmatia had not yet been fully consolidated, and trade in the Serbian lands was concentrated in the hands of Dubrovnik, against which its powerful rival could not compete at that time.

By the end of the 13th and the beginning of the 14th century Venetian influence over the Slavs of the Adriatic had increased. After the submission of Zadar, Dubrovnik recognised its dependence on Venice, an example followed by the main towns and islands of the Adriatic; in 1278 Hvar and Brach, in 1322 Shibenik and Trogir, and in 1327 Split, and in 1329 Nin. The increasing political and commercial power of Venice naturally led to a greater development of direct trade with the Serbian lands. The number of Venetian merchants visiting these areas increased significantly though trade in these territories was not without its dangers. Both as strangers and perhaps equally important as Catholics, merchants were subject to arrest and all kinds of oppression. Thus in Bosnia up to 50 merchants were arrested in 1300 for whom Venice had to plead through the mediation of Dubrovnik. So far as the kingdom of Serbia is concerned there is evidence from Venice touching the years between 1286 and 1318 that Venetian merchants suffered frequent harassment. In spite of these difficulties, however, commercial links between Serbia and Venice were strengthening. Nevertheless Dubrovnik remained in general master of all Serbian trade, as is evident from a resolution of the Great Council which talks of 'containing the subjects of Venice (homines de Venetiis)'. All attempts to break the trade of Dubrovnik failed. The Venetians made use of their supreme rights and took upon themselves the defence of Dubrovnik's interests throughout the Serbian lands as an indirect way of breaking the near monopoly of the trade which Dubrovnik enjoyed with the Serbian crown. Politically it led Venice to enter into closer relations with Dushan. Under Milutin petitions from Venice were concerned almost exclusively with Dubrovnik. Milutin did not regard Venetian merchants highly and they did not enjoy his protection, being frequently arrested and detained by the natives. Under Decanski relations between Venice and Serbia improved, though the King was concerned at the growing strength of Venice in Dalmatia. In May 1330 Decanski granted to Venetian merchants the right to trade freely in the Serbian lands and free passage through the kingdom to the Byzantine Empire, apart from Bulgaria, because the King was planning a war against Tsar Michael. In general, however, relations between Venice and Serbia were not particularly close.

The attitude of Venice changed as a result of the establishment of the Serbian Empire and the Republic attempted to enter into closer relations with Dushan. Dushan was above all anxious to obtain arms from Venice, along with luxury goods considered essential for the court, in return for which he was prepared to grant privileges to Venetian merchants throughout the Serbian lands. The strengthening of commercial relations posed the question of a close political alliance with the aim of combined action against Byzantium. On the occasion of Dushan's marriage with Helen, the sister of Alexander of Bulgaria, delegates from Dubrovnik and Venice attended the ceremony. In June of that year the Venetian Senate met to discuss the selling of arms to Serbia. The Serbian ambassador was required to give an assurance that these arms were for the personal use of the King 'quod predicta omnia sint tantum et propria dicti regis'. The Senate made it clear to Dushan that they were doing him a favour in allowing him to purchase arms; nevertheless scarcely a year passed without Dushan turning to Venice. Arms and war materials were particularly essential in view of the continual fighting in which he was involved. In view of the 'favours' they were granting him it was inevitable that Venice should demand certain favours in return. These included a request that a special court should be set up for their merchants in Serbia; this was conceded by Dushan. At the same time they requested measures for the security of their merchants in the lands controlled by Dushan. It is clear that merchants had suffered harassment from the native population, for we find Dushan assuring the Doge that a certain robber who had captured a Venetian merchant would be caught without fail and all measures taken to give complete satisfaction for the losses incurred by the unfortunate merchant. These promises were not fulfilled. The Venetian merchant did not receive compensation, probably because the guilty party was not captured and the King could not or did not wish to pay the large sum demanded in compensation from his own treasury. The Venetians retaliated by imposing a temporary ban on their merchants visiting Kotor. But restrictions on trade with Serbia were not to their advantage. In the end they were able to reach agreement with Dushan which would ensure adequate protection for their merchants in Serbia.

Kotor, the only one of the Dalmatian Councils in the possession of the Serbian state, though long enjoying self-government, was an important centre of direct commerce between Serbia and foreign merchants. Its magnificent bay and advantageous geographical position made it after Dubrovnik one of the most important commercial centres on the eastern coast of the Adriatic. There Venice established a depot for goods destined for Serbia. In 1335 they were granted equal rights with the citizens of Kotor. Responsibility for unlawful payments and the satisfaction of creditors was, by agreement of 1335, granted not only to native purchasers but all those in friendly alliance as so-called friendly brothers (po bratimstvo). Special mention in the agreement was made of the Venetians who had been robbed, and indicated the powerful influence of Venice in Serbia. In 1336 the Senate gave permission for emissaries from Serbia to export arms to the value of 30 *funts;* the explanation for this request for arms lies in the fact that Dushan had begun a campaign in Albania. In the same year the Senate gave permission for the transit through its territory of 300 cavalry hired, probably in Italy, by Dushan for his personal defence.

In 1340, having achieved some military successes in the south, Dushan made a serious attempt to conclude an alliance with Venice. He 'visibly crawled' to the Republic, stressing the value he placed on Venetian friendship and his long-standing desire for a closer relationship between

Venice and Serbia. He also requested that he be made an honorary citizen of Venice; there was an important reason for what might seem an odd request. In the course of his conquests he had made many enemies – never was his position as king assured. It might be that circumstances would force him to seek refuge in Venice and if he were a citizen he could live there as of right with his family and, equally could freely make a necessary escape when and if circumstances were propitious. To what extent internal opposition existed is difficult to guage; as a successful war leader he enjoyed strong support and he was surrounded by influential people such as Oliver. It is more likely that in making the request for citizenship he was simply flattering the Venetians the more easily to obtain agreement for an alliance. He claimed to have heard that a movement against Venice was developing in Dalmatia which was ready to seize Zadar. The military preparations in Hungary constituted a threat to Venice; he, Dushan was prepared to put 500 cavalry at their disposal. Moreover he was ready if required, personally at the head of an army to come to the aid of Venice 'personalite cum nostro exercitu in vestrum juvenem et auxilium interesse'. Finally he stated that the commercial interests of Venice were as dear as his own, and he was prepared to guarantee the complete security of merchants travelling through his territories to the Byzantine Empire and Constantinople; should any losses be incurred compensation would be paid from the royal treasury. In his letter containing these favourable proposals he begged the Doge to send an emissary to whom he would confirm all the proposals contained in the letter 'excelentiar vestre placeat ad nos aliquem virum nobilem destinare'. To this he added another request; having recovered from a serious illness which had threatened his life, he wished to fulfil a vow made when his life was in danger, 'when his doctor had lost all hope', of building a monastery in the name of the Saviour in Jerusalem. It was intended to send some leaders with a great sum of money and Dushan expressed the wish that the Venetians would lend him two ships furnished at his expense to transport the leaders to the island of Cyprus, stating that there was no-one else he would wish to turn to.

The courteous and diplomatic manner in which the Senate responded to Dushan's request could not conceal the fact that they were rejecting it. While they were prepared to grant him citizenship and refuge for his family, this was conditional on his accepting the obligations of a citizen necessary for the security of the State; clearly as a citizen of Venice he would enjoy no special privileges. The Senate expressed their thanks for his offer of military help; if necessary they would make use of it. But there was no mention of an alliance. The promise to protect Venetian merchants was welcomed but the Senate gave him to understand that they would not be satisfied with verbal assurances. They ignored Dushan's request to despatch an emissary to

Serbia for the purpose of concluding negotiations and failed to respond to his request for ships for the journey to Cyprus. They implied that the King should be thankful that his request for Venetian citizenship had not been rejected. The Venetians were well aware that they had something that Dushan required and were determined to extract the maximum advantages in the shape of commercial privileges. In the following years relations between Dushan and Venice were confined to minor matters. The purchase of arms continued although the Venetians were not always willing to supply all that was demanded and did not permit the recruitment of soldiers. All this was done to impress on Dushan his dependence on Venice.

Meanwhile Dushan was preparing to take advantage of the continuing civil unrest in the Byzantine Empire. The situation there was a matter of concern for Venice. It was not in the interests of the Republic that the kingdom of Serbia should be strengthened at the expense of the feeble Empire, which might damage the commercial interests of the Venetians. At the same time, dissatisfaction with Venetian rule in Dalmatia was growing; opposition was particularly strong in Zadar. The Ban of Bosnia and other Slav rulers were constricting Venetian power in the Adriatic. The aim of the Hungarian king to restore Dalmatia to his rule forced the Venetians to look more favourably at an alliance with Dushan. The government in Constantinople, aware of the Venetian influence on Dushan, pleaded with them to exercise their influence to persuade the Serbian ruler to withdraw his support for Cantacuzene. In 1343 a Venetian ambassador arrived at the court of the King; his mission was to establish peace between Serbians and Greeks, and to sound out Dushan about his offer of protection for the 'Venetian rulers in Slavonia' who were being threatened by the Ban of Bosnia and other 'barons of Slavonia'. This mission was successful; Dushan broke with Cantacuzene and established friendly relations with the party of the Empress Anna. A proposal to marry his son Urosh to the sister of the Emperor, however, came to nothing.

Faced with the Hungarian threat to Dalmatia, the Venetians began to take active measures. They concluded peace negotiations with the Croatian princes and drew up a project for a general alliance of all Veneto-Dalmatian cities with the rulers of Croatia, Bosnia and Serbia. The project was unsuccessful; only some of the princes such as Mladin of Croatia, and some of the islands were prepared to co-operate with Venice. In the meantime the Hungarians had already moved into Dalmatia; Knin fell into their hands and in 1342 Zadar. Dushan meanwhile, despite his rapprochement with the Palaeologi, continued his military activity in Macedonia, and by 1346 was master of Serres. Encouraged by his latest successes he was determined more than ever to win the co-operation of Venice for joint action against the Empire. The difficulties the Venetians were experiencing in the Adriatic strengthened his belief that they would now be prepared to enter into a military alliance with Serbia. As an inducement he began by agreeing to re-open negotiations over the rights of the Venetians in Kotor, promising that the general commercial interests of Venice would be completely protected there and in all other territories of his domain. Dushan then turned to the city of Zadar which had 'rashly and impudently risen against you (the Venetians)'. He expressed surprise at the failure of the Doge to inform him of this event and was ready to send part of his army or indeed all of his strength (aut in copiam) to aid them. Dushan failed to realise that the Venetians, however anxious they were to restore their power and influence in the Adriatic, were unwilling to place themselves under an obligation to a power whose ambitions – the destruction of the Byzantine Empire – clashed with their aims. On the other hand Dushan was too powerful to be slighted; he now styled himself 'Stephanus dei gratiia Servie, Dioclia, Chilminie (Hum), Zante, Albanie et Maritume rex – totius imperii Romanie dominus'. The proposals of the King would have to be treated with respect, a situation requiring all the political skill and diplomatic finesse of which the Venetians were masters. Otherwise that strength which the long list of titles symbolised might be turned against them. In their answer the Venetians expressed their thanks to Dushan for his friendship, accepted with gracious approval his proposals for discussions on Kotor, and permitted the sale of arms to Serbia. While refusing the offer of military help, they softened their refusal with flattering references to the close friendship between the King and the Republic; if the need arose they would be happy to turn to their friend for help. The rebellious Zadar would soon get the punishment it deserved. In fact the Venetians were worried at the possibility of Zadar finding allies among the Slav princes of Croatia and Dalmatia or a forced settlement at their expense. The time had come for Dushan openly to declare his intentions.

In February 1346 a Serbian emissary again arrived in Venice bringing news of Dushan's coronation as Emperor, and proposing in the name of the new Emperor a joint military alliance directed against the Byzantine Empire. At the same time the emissary expressed the readiness of his Emperor to act as intermediary to bring about a reconciliation between Venice and Zadar. The Venetians still prevaricated; while expressing their congratulations and the hope that the Emperor's power and glory would increase, they rejected the proposed alliance, giving as reason for rejection the fact that they were involved in war with Zadar; secondly they were bound by oath to agreement with Byzantium and to break this would be a sin against 'God and man'! Likewise they were unable to accept Dushan's offer of mediation since Zadar could not assent to this without the permission of the Hungarian king. The rebels would assume that it was

Venice that had called for mediation, which would be flattering to the former and weaken the Venetian position.

Behind all the excuses put forward the simple fact was that Venice did not want an alliance, but also wished to avoid offending Dushan. Venice was in a difficult position in 1346. The greater the danger to their rule in Dalmatia, the more necessary it was to conserve their strength for a war against Zadar, and they could spare neither troops, ships or money for a war against Byzantium from which the benefits, if any, would accrue to Dushan. The rebels in Zadar were supported by Hungary and the Croatian princes, and were able to maintain their resistance throughout 1346. Dushan failed to understand why Venice, in such circumstances, was not prepared to take advantage of the help offered by Serbia. It was in fact the power of Dushan that they feared; they wanted to maintain friendly relations to ensure their commercial advantages without strengthening Serbian power. Hence the refusal of Dushan's offer of mediation; such an offer seemed an insult to their prestige. Nevertheless some months previously they had without loss of dignity concluded an alliance with the Ban of Bosnia and agreed to his mediation with Zadar. Relations between Dushan and Venice remained friendly; Dushan continued his military action against Byzantium and turned to the Venetians for arms which the latter, though unwillingly, could not refuse him.

In July 1346 Dushan once more offered to mediate and this time the offer was accepted. It is probable that the Venetians realised that the real enemy was Hungary; the Senate suggested that a meeting between Dushan and the King of Hungary would be in the interests of Venice. They turned directly to Dushan for help and advice for the Venetian plenipotentiaries sent by Venice to negotiate with Hungary. The siege of Zadar was failing; if the city was not to be finally lost, a speedy reconciliation with Hungary was essential. Louis of Hungary, however, did not receive the Venetian ambassadors, nor did the proposed meeting with Dushan take place. When the Venetians finally sought the help of Dushan it was too late; seeking a meeting with the Emperor to discuss the question of avoiding a war with Bosnia, the Venetian ambassador found that Dushan was no longer in Serbia, but deep in Byzantine territory 'infra terram in partibus Romaniae'.

The conquest of Constantinople remained the ultimate objective of Dushan; for that he required a fleet which only Venice could provide. The rejection of the proposed alliance meant the postponement of the project. He resolved to annex those lands in the south still under Byzantine rule; Epirus, Vlach and Thessaly, these being lands ruled by the family of Cantacuzene. In the autumn of 1346 he advanced on Epirus, the northern part of which he had already conquered; by the following year all lands west of Pindar were in his hands. John Cantacuzene had now been proclaimed

Emperor, but faced with strong internal opposition, was in no position to provide help to his relations in the lands threatened by Dushan. The Albanians, seizing the southern areas of the peninsula, made up the main part of Dushan's army, and made a major contribution to the conquest of these lands. The inability of the governors of these provinces to protect the mainly Greek population, led many of the latter to join with the invaders. This may have saved their lives; it is unlikely that it preserved their possessions.

Cantacuzene reproached Dushan for the destruction he had caused and the hunger and misery of the population which had forced them 'willingly to give themselves as slaves to the barbarians rather than die of hunger'. Dushan's half brother Simeon was appointed as Despot of Etoli and Arkan. Prior to their conquest by Dushan these territories had been ruled by the despot Anna Palaeologus; Simeon was married to her daughter, while Anna herself was the wife of the despot Oliver, brother-in-law of Dushan, who was entrusted with the territories of Kanin and Belgrade in central Albania. It may be that by arranging such marriages Dushan hoped to compensate the Greek population for the suffering they had endured at the hands of the Albanians who were too fierce even for him to control.

The victories of the Serbian armies in the south naturally alarmed the Venetians; the establishment of a powerful government in the peninsula, gradually eliminating Byzantium as a serious factor, was detrimental to their interests. Ideally the best solution for Venice was either the restoration of the Latin Empire, or the maintenance of the weak Emperor who could be bullied into granting concessions – in other words a Venetian puppet. At the same time they felt themselves threatened by the Angevin rulers on the mainland and the islands of Cefalonia, Zakinth, Levkad and Ithaca which were coveted by Venice. Nevertheless they were still supplying arms to Dushan in 1348. In the same year Dushan again attempted to conclude an alliance with them. In a letter, signing himself Emperor of the Greeks 'Stephanus dei gratia Graecorum imperator' he expressed his willingness to resume commercial negotiations over Kotor. In addition he made a new offer to mediate between Venice and the Hungarians, and concluded by asking for three armed galleys. Relations between Venice and Louis of Hungary remained hostile, Zadar was forced to submit to Venice without diminishing the threat to Venetian domination in Dalmatia. The Senate therefore accepted 'with satisfaction' the mediation of Dushan in the hope, no doubt, that Dushan, himself a threat to Hungary, might be able to wring concessions from Louis. Even now, however, they were not prepared to commit themselves fully to Dushan; he was offered ships but not permitted to arm them in Venice. He was reminded that it was not the custom of the Republic to offer privileges to all and sundry. The purchase of ships suggests that Dushan was planning to attack Constantinople and had given up hope of Venetian co-operation.

Serbian armies advanced on Vlach and Thessaly; the governor of these provinces had no prospect of receiving reinforcements from the Emperor and died after the loss of Epirus and Akarnin. A strong Albanian force under the leadership of Prilep advanced on Thessaly. In January the Venetians congratulated the Emperor on his latest achievements and entrusted him with the defence of Pteli and other Venetian territories now in his possession. Dushan granted Prilep the title of Despot and established him as ruler of the conquered territories. Cantacuzene was engaged at that time in a difficult and, from the point of view of Byzantium, largely unsuccessful war against the Genoese who were firmly established in Galatea. He was in no position to provide help to areas so far removed from the capital and almost completely surrounded by enemy forces. The relatively easy conquest encouraged Dushan to attempt the final conquest of Byzantium.

Following his military successes, Dushan summoned a Council consisting of the Patriarch and archbishops and nobles to Skopje to work out a Code of Law – the Zakonik. Dushan's rule now extended over non-Serbians: Greeks, Bulgarians and Vlachs, and it is possible that he saw himself as the successor of Justinian as a law giver. As we shall see, Dushan was anxious to conciliate the Greeks in particular, and this is illustrated by the Code. The Code so to speak set the seal on his conquests in Thessaly in the same way as the establishment of the Patriarchate and his coronation as Emperor marked his annexation of Macedonia. The promulgation of the Code implies the decision of Dushan to organise and consolidate his empire by unifying the component parts. The Code was a written expression of common law and custom which defined the political and social basis of the Empire. Dushan, however, was still obsessed with the capture of Constantinople, and had neither the time, nor was he willing to concern himself with the consolidation of the Empire he had won. Once the Code had been published he advanced against Salonika, the only city of Macedonia which had maintained its independence in spite of repeated assaults. The second city of the Byzantine Empire, no longer recognising the authority of Constantinople, was in a state of anarchy. The Serbian army sat down to besiege the city while Dushan entered into negotiations with the citizens in an attempt to persuade them to hand it over. The Zealots, the party controlling the city, who had been heavily bribed by Dushan, won over many of the citizens to hand over the city but Dushan was never able to take Salonika.

In the following year he made a further attempt to conclude an effective alliance with Venice but the attempt proved fruitless. The period of easy victories was coming to an end; by 1349 he had reached the height of his power. It was becoming more and more evident that the capture of Constantinople would not be as easy as his conquest of the defenceless provinces; in any case he lacked the means for an assault against the city. The creation of a Serbo-Greek Empire could not be achieved without the aid of a Venetian fleet. The growing power of Dushan, however, was becoming a matter of concern to Venice; the rule of the Republic in Negropont and Pteli, bordering on Serbian territory, was threatened by Prilep. The object of Venetian policy was to limit rather than strengthen Dushan's power. For the moment the Byzantine Empire was necessary to Venice; the Venetians were preparing for war against the Genoese and their colony at Galatea, and counted on concluding an alliance with Cantacuzene. The Senate instructed their ambassador, travelling through Serbia to discuss matters of trade, to persuade Dushan to make peace with Cantacuzene. In the event of Dushan agreeing to such a proposal, the ambassador should immediately communicate this agreement to the Venetian plenipotentiary in Constantinople, or, if necessary, should travel himself to the capital. Dushan rejected the Venetian proposal. From his point of view, peace with Cantacuzene would imply the abandonment of his long term aims and possibly the restoration of some at least of his conquests. He was unlikely to agree to a negotiated peace when, after a series of military successes, final victory appeared to be within his grasp.

The rejection of their proposal by Dushan led the Venetians to come to an agreement with Cantacuzene; when Dushan received news of this agreement he realised that the Venetians were pursuing their own interests, which were directly contrary to his own, and no help could be expected from them. Nevertheless he persisted in his negotiations. These negotiations indicate the 'political stupidity' of Dushan in sharp contrast to the political skill of the Venetians. In rejecting these proposals the Venetians did so in such a way as to maintain friendly relations with him for their advantage. Dushan's proposals contained 11 points. The first of these contained a suggestion for a meeting between him and the Doge. He then requested Venetian citizenship for himself and his family and all his descendents, which if granted would entitle him to complete security. This was an unusual request for a successful ruler to make and it may be that he was simply flattering the Venetians. In the event of his being forced to reside in Venice, he and his family should be treated according to their rank. For his part the Emperor was prepared to provide military help to the Republic; on the other hand the Venetians should be ready to provide him with men and ships if required. As he had conquered 10 parts of the 'Roman' Empire (decem partes Romanie imperii Constantinopalitanti) apart from the capital which he was unable to subdue, Venice should supply him with ships and men for that purpose. In the event of the capital falling, all the despotates should be returned to Venice. If these inducements were not acceptable, he was ready with the help of ships supplied by Venice to attack the Genoese colony of Galatea. Since the Genoese were the principal rivals of the Venetians, such a proposal would have obvious attractions for them. Dushan then claimed that his objective was to free John Palaeologus from the hands of the usurper Cantacuzene. Turning to the question of trade, Dushan was prepared to offer trading rights and privileges to Venetian merchants in Serbia in return for reciprocal rights for Serbians trading in Venetian territory; as an earnest of his goodwill he despatched 1,200 *perpers* to Venice in compensation for the loss of goods suffered by Venetian merchants in his territories.

Failing to obtain agreement to an alliance against Byzantium, Dushan was anxious at least to ensure the neutrality of Venice in the event of his being involved in war. In return he promised neutrality if Venice should find itself at war with another power. He agreed to make peace with Bosnia provided the Ban returned all lands captured from the Serbians and paid compensation for the damage inflicted on Serbian citizens. Venice reacted coolly to these proposals, the majority of which they rejected. The offer of a meeting between Dushan and the Doge was declined on the grounds that the latter was debarred by law from leaving Venice. The Republic was ready to offer Venetian citizenship to the Emperor and his family and treat them in a manner befitting their rank, and accepted in a vague way his offer of help. They were not prepared to grant any trading rights to Serbians. Enough of Dushan's proposals were accepted to ensure the continuation of friendly relations with Serbia, but since at that time relations between Venice and Byzantium were close, acceptance of Dushan's proposal for a combined attack against the Empire to which the Venetians were bound by oath would be a reflection on their honour. The concessions the Venetians were prepared to make to ensure the continuance of friendly relations with Dushan cost them nothing, particularly the granting of Venetian citizenship to the Emperor and his family. In finally agreeing to the proposals regarding trade the Venetians gained more than the Serbians, for their trade with Serbia was greater than that of the Serbians with Venice. The conciliatory tone of the reply to the proposals of Dushan did not conceal the fact that a combined attack by the two powers against Constantinople was rejected.

It may be inferred that the Venetians were not restrained by questions of national honour but by the risks involved in such an undertaking. Besides as businessmen they preferred to achieve their aims by negotiations rather than squander their resources on an undertaking whose outcome was uncertain and the advantages doubtful. Before they reached Constantinople they would have to defeat the Genoese in Galatea, and they believed this could be achieved more easily in alliance with Byzantium. Any attempt to attack Constantinople would meet with strong resistance from the Greeks on religious grounds – in this respect Dushan had the advantage of belonging to the Orthodox Church – and from the Turks who were a new factor in the situation. Dushan consistently failed to grasp the fact that the long term aims of Venice could not be reconciled with his own ambitions so far as these were concerned with Constantinople. Apart from the war with Genoa, the Venetians were concerned over the Hungarian threat in Dalmatia. The compensation which Dushan offered in return for an alliance could, they believed, be obtained by less dangerous means. In the event of a successful war against Genoa they counted on obtaining Galatea from the grateful Emperor once the Genoese had been driven out. The Despotate of Epirus, offered them by Dushan as an inducement, they hoped to obtain by diplomacy.

The inability of Dushan to understand Venetian policy is evident from the fact that an ambassador 'domini regis Rascie' arrived in Venice 'petentis auxilium nostrum contra imperium Romanie' which the Venetians rejected 'excusando nos a dicta requestione sua', a final and categorical reply to Dushan's proposals. The confirmation of his Venetian citizenship which followed shortly after may have been intended to compensate for the rejection of his proposals. This finally seems to have convinced Dushan of the futility of attempting to create an anti-Byzantine alliance at least for the present. The break between Serbia and Venice was not complete. In the first place a break would threaten Venetian trade with Serbia; more important the Hungarian threat in Dalmatia made it desirable to keep on good terms with Dushan, the only power in the Balkans in a position to resist Hungary.

In 1350 the Venetians launched an attack against the Genoese. About the same time Dushan, in a move suggesting a temporary abandonment of his plans against Constantinople, turned west and prepared to attack Salonika, counting on the support of the Zealots, which led the anti-Serbian parties in the city to the decision to get rid of all 'foreigners' i.e. Serbians, for which reason they called on Cantacuzene for support. The attempt to capture Salonika was abandoned; Dushan was aware that the city could not be captured without a fleet. It is possible that the object was to annoy the Venetians.

From the proposals made to Venice and the Venetian response there is reference to the discord between Dushan and the Ban of Bosnia. This was a matter which deeply concerned Venice; the Venetians counted on Bosnia as an ally against Hungary. Hence from their point of view the Ban was fighting the wrong enemy. At the same time they were concerned over the threat from Dushan against Dubrovnik and other possessions in Dalmatia. A Serbian victory over Bosnia might encourage Dushan to attack these territories. Venice could not feel safe until the Serbian armies had been withdrawn from the west; consequently the Venetians exercised all their diplomatic skill to effect a reconciliation between Dushan and Bosnia. The main pretext for hostilities lay in the alleged seizure by the Ban of some border areas of Serbia. In discussion with Venice, Dushan expressed his readiness to establish peace with Bosnia provided the Ban was prepared to compensate him for the damage to Serbia.

Reconciliation with Bosnia was the price he was willing to pay for an alliance with Venice, and the Venetians as we have seen had rejected his proposals. Relations between Serbia and Bosnia remained strained and since there was nothing apparently that the Venetians were prepared to offer in return for peace with Bosnia, preparations were made for war. According to one source Dushan invaded with a force of 80,000 troops 'il quale aveva gia masso guerra al Bano ed era entrato con esercito di ottanta milla uomimi in Bossian'. In view of the number of troops at his disposal, some would have to be withdrawn from other areas; in fact Macedonia and Albania were left virtually undefended. The army was withdrawn from Salonika and only token forces remained in the fortified towns – Verri for example had only 1,500 troops. The defenceless state of the conquered territories was an encouragement to Cantacuzene to launch an attack. Lacking the necessary strength, however, he attempted to negotiate with Dushan; when these negotiations broke down he turned to the Osman Turks who had already provided help for him in the civil war. Dushan was well aware of the Turkish threat; in 1347 an army of 10,000 Turks had seized and pillaged the eastern parts of the Serbian Empire. When Cantacuzene received a request from the 'patriots' of Salonika to seize the city he again turned to the Turks. Suleman was ready with an army of 20,000 men; the threat was only averted by the recall of the Turks to Asia Minor, and instead of pillaging Serbia they turned to Bulgaria. But the danger had not passed. Twenty-two ships carrying a small army reached the shores of Macedonia; with their help Cantacuzene advanced towards Salonika, was recognised as Emperor, and drove the Serbian garrisons from the fortified towns. Those who had not fled to prepared positions were captured.

Taking advantage of Dushan's absence and the defenceless state of the eastern areas of the Serbian Empire, Cantacuzene was able to conquer south-west Macedonia, all Boetia, and penetrated Albania and Thessaly. The credit for these victories belongs mainly to the Turks who ravaged the territories up to Skopje and terrorised the Serbian rulers into submission to Cantacuzene, leading some of them, temporarily to join him. Cantacuzene's assertion that these Serbian rulers were dissatisfied with Dushan's rule must be treated with scepticism. It was natural that the withdrawal of troops from Macedonia for the campaign in Bosnia should cause a certain amount of resentment, but it is an exaggeration to claim as he does that the situation in Skopje was hopeless and that the city was ready to submit to him. Skopje was now a purely Serbian city; while it is possible that Cantacuzene could capture it, it is difficult to believe in a voluntary surrender. Nor is it likely that Dushan would have refused to send aid as Cantacuzene claims. The fact that some Serbians switched allegiance from Dushan to Cantacuzene was not due to a belief in the latter's aims but simply in furtherance of their own ends.

One example is that of Volk or Vuk, who gave a false oath to Cantacuzene, but abandoned him when Dushan returned to save his commander. Edessa alone had to be taken by force; all others yielded voluntarily. But the acquisition of these towns marked the limit of Cantacuzene's success; the attempt to capture the inaccessible fortresses of Serbia, thus penning up the route to the interior of Thessaly, was a failure. His principal allies the Turks, pillaged far and wide, and abandoned him for richer pastures, and with the small remaining forces at his disposal he could do little. Withdrawing from Verri he finally returned to Salonika.

The disturbing news from Macedonia forced Dushan to withdraw from Bosnia and he advanced to the south-eastern part of his empire. The results of the Turkish invasion must have created a disagreeable impression. In view of the unfinished business in Bosnia he was ready for reconciliation with Cantacuzene provided this could be achieved without the necessity of ceding any of the captured towns. Negotiations on such terms could not be acceptable to Cantacuzene, and fighting continued, resulting in the loss of nearly all the territories Cantacuzene had recovered. For Dushan this was not difficult. His forces were recalled from Bosnia and Cantacuzene, realising the weakness of his position, refrained from active hostilities. Leaving his son-in-law John Palaeologus in Salonika, he succeeded in making his way back to Constantinople where fresh difficulties awaited him. After his departure Dushan besieged Edessa; the town was forced to surrender and was subject to frightful pillaging after its fall. In the summer of 1351 Dushan was able to return to the west to continue the war with Bosnia. One significant event is witness to the extent of Dushan's reconquest of Macedonia. At a Church Council to condemn the teachings of Barlaam and Akindin, only the bishops of Thrace took part because, according to the witness of Gregoras, apart from Thrace no other territory remained in the Empire.

The success of Cantacuzene had been short lived; nevertheless in the eyes of Dushan it must have seemed very important. The obstacles facing him on the road to Constantinople were more formidable than they had appeared at one time. He saw Cantacuzene still as a dangerous enemy; above all he was aware of the growing power of the Turks, the ostensible allies of

Cantacuzene. To the memory of the rout at Stephiano there was added the powerful impression of the destruction and pillaging carried out by those 'barbarians' in Macedonia. It is true that the Turkish action in Macedonia was not carried out in conjunction with Cantacuzene; limited attacks and looting were carried out by them in Thessaly as well as in Macedonia. Nevertheless this was small consolation to Dushan, and must have been particularly worrying as was the Turkish attack in Bulgaria. He was still not convinced of the impossibility of receiving help from Venice in his struggle against the Empire. At the moment when Cantacuzene seized Salonika, the Venetians expressed their willingness to take part in a war against the Genoese. In 1351 and 1352 they openly appeared as allies of Byzantium, and Dushan realised the futility of further attempts to win them to his side.

None of the obstacles was formidable enough to turn Dushan from his dream of conquering the whole Empire of Byzantium. His first idea was to enter into friendly relations with the Turks, attracting them from Cantacuzene and winning them over to his side, using the methods of Cantacuzene himself, who had sacrificed his own daughter for this purpose. Dushan regarded himself as a powerful emperor in no way inferior to Cantacuzene, 'illegally' occupying the throne of Constantinople, and considered that a family alliance with him would persuade the 'infidel' to recognise the honour and advantage which would accrue to him from such a union. He proposed, therefore, that his daughter should marry one of the sons of the Turkish leader. The Turks were in agreement with this proposal and an emissary was sent to conclude negotiations and resolve the question of marriage. But the meeting was not destined to take place; Cantacuzene was able to prevent it, though at great sacrifice to himself and the Empire. The Turkish emissaries on the way to meet the Serbians at Rodos were attacked by the son-in-law of Cantacuzene, the former Despot of Epirus, Nicephor. One was killed, the other was captured. Ohran was furious at this indignity. He broke with Cantacuzene, laid waste Thrace and threatened Constantinople. Nevertheless Cantacuzene had achieved his aim; there was no more talk of a renewal of relations between Dushan and Ohran. A year later Cantacuzene was able to restore relations with the Turks. Politically Dushan was no match for Cantacuzene. However, while both believed they were making use of the Turks, the opposite was the case.

The responsibility for the Turkish settlement in the Balkans has generally been attributed to Cantacuzene. The facts are usually presented in such a way as to suggest that the Emperor summoned the Turks to support him against his personal enemies and the enemies of the State, while Dushan is depicted as the warrior gallantly defending Christianity against Islam. This is not a tenable view. The successful raids carried out by the Turks obviously encouraged them to launch more massive attacks and take advantage of the disunity in the Balkans. Finally in none of the actions of the rulers and peoples of this period, with their limited outlook, was there any awareness of the real nature of the Turkish threat; on the contrary, each of them tried to reach agreement with the Turks, and Cantacuzene was not alone in this. If, indeed it is irrefutable that Cantacuzene established relations with the Turks, both Venice and Genoa, these stout defenders of Christianity, were equally prepared to enter into alliance with the 'infidel'. One need only recall the war between Venice and Genoa in 1351 and 1352 when both sides loaded the Turkish leader with gifts in an effort to obtain Turkish support. Dushan too saw the Turks as potential allies, not as a dangerous threat. The evidence shows no justification for regarding Dushan as a conscious fighter against the 'infidel'; he was no more far sighted than the others. Clashes when they occurred generally came about by accident. On the contrary he sought alliance with them, counting in this way on saving his empire from devastation on the one hand while obtaining their help against the Emperor on the other. This does not, of course, justify Cantacuzene, but merely shows that he shared the guilt with others. Perhaps Dushan would not have co-operated with the Turks had he realised the consequences for his own empire as well as for Byzantium, but like most rulers he seldom looked beyond the immediate future.

While he was considering the possibility of alliance with the Turks, he was tempted to intervene in the civil war which was again threatening to erupt in the Empire. The party of the Palaeologi, defending the rights of the young Emperor, and taking advantage of the difficulties of Cantacuzene, were preparing for open rebellion. In that case Dushan was ready to intervene; by supporting the party of the legitimate Emperor he believed it would be easier for him to penetrate Thrace and attack Constantinople. Moving from Macedonia at the beginning of 1351, Cantacuzene abandoned John Palaeologus in Salonika. The adherents of the young Emperor immediately entered into relations with Dushan who proceeded to Salonika with his wife. The full details of the negotiations have not been preserved, but the gist of them was that John Palaeologus should abandon his wife and marry the sister-in-law of Dushan, the latter's daughter being considered as a bride for the son of Ohran. Just as Cantacuzene thought to strengthen his position by a marriage alliance with the family of the Palaeologi, so Dushan believed that a similar alliance on his part would give him a legal right to intervene in the civil war for his own ends. The Empress Anna, sent by Cantacuzene to Salonika, was able to persuade her son to break off relations with Dushan, and the Emperor, reconciled with Cantacuzene, returned to Constantinople. Dushan and his wife left Salonika according to Cantacuzene 'in great shame'; he did not renew the siege of the city, nor did he make any move to Thrace. Evidently he considered the first useless in view of the impossibility of conquering the well-defended Salonika, and the second operation he considered too risky at that period. He decided to wait until the agreement between Cantacuzene and Palaeologus had broken down and then attempt an offensive. The opportunity came in the following year.

In 1352 the civil war in the Byzantine Empire was in full swing. Chalcidic and the valley of the Maritsa suffered grievous destruction at the hands of both combatants. Finally Cantacuzene with the aid of the Turks began to achieve superiority over Palaeologus who was forced to turn to Dushan and Bulgaria. Dushan accepted the propositions of the Emperor, but stipulated that the latter's brother should be sent to Serbia as a hostage. When agreement had been reached on this point he sent a small force to help the Emperor. This was prudent; in spite of all the temptation which the conquest of Thrace and Constantinople represented, he decided not to commit all his forces to intervention but to limit himself to the sending of one army leader. The Turks under the leadership of Cantacuzene presented a formidable force and the outcome of a clash with the latter was too uncertain to gamble the whole of his empire. If Palaeologus was successful he could claim his reward for the support he had provided; if on the other hand Cantacuzene was finally victorious he could without too much loss withdraw and still be strong enough to negotiate with the victor.

At a meeting between the Serbians and Bulgarians with John Palaeologus at Dimotok it was agreed that part of the Greek army should attack the fortress of Empith, held by Cantacuzene. The Slavs took up position on the banks of the River Maritsa with the intention of moving to the attack on the following morning. The Bulgarian army lay nearer the town than the Serbians. Neither was aware that a force of 20,000 Turkish cavalry under the command of Suleman, summoned by Cantacuzene from Asia, was near. The Turks had crossed the Hellespont, hurried to Cantacuzene and pitched their camp by night on the banks of the Maritsa. The allies were no match for the Turks. The Bulgarians were able to flee in the direction of Dimitok leaving the Serbians and Greeks to bear the brunt of the fighting. The Turks outnumbered the Serbians, were better armed, had speedier and hardier horses, while the Serbians on their clumsy horses could not manoeuvre against the enemy. Crushed and scattered by the Turkish onslaught those who saved themselves on the battlefield were captured in flight. Some of the Greeks were able to find safety in Dimitok. The Turks then returned to Adrianople, after which they devastated Bulgaria before returning to Asia Minor.

This disaster, an account of which would be transmitted to Dushan, must have made it clear that the Turks were the main enemy. Dushan had three options: first he could try to separate the Turks from Cantacuzene;

secondly he could persuade them to join him; thirdly he could create an army powerful enough to defeat them. Cantacuzene without the Turks could be defeated. So far as the second option was concerned, experience suggested that the Turks were as dangerous as allies as enemies. From the military point of view Serbian resources were probably strained to the limit. When Cantacuzene appeared shortly after the Battle of Maritsa in the Morea and Chalcidic to exact revenge for the fall of these provinces to Palaeologus, Dushan did not take advantage of the proximity of his enemy to engage him in battle. One reason for his inactivity was probably the threat from Hungary whose king was trying to win support from the West for a Crusade against Dushan on the alleged grounds of heresy. Reluctantly, therefore, Dushan had to be satisfied with what he had achieved in 1350.

In 1354 as the civil war within the Byzantine Empire intensified and the Turks, established in Gallipoli, began to threaten other parts of Thrace, a party emerged in Constantinople which saw no other way out of the desperate situation except to reject both Cantacuzene and Palaeologus and submit to a foreign ruler. There were those who were ready to unite with the Serbian Empire. The Venetian *bailey* in Constantinople in August 1354 informed the Doge that in view of the defenceless state of the Empire against the Turks, Byzantium was prepared to recognise the King of Hungary or the Serbian Emperor if the Venetians were not willing to take over the government of the Empire. The Venetian plenipotentiary argued strongly in favour of Venice, promising help not only against the Turks but also against the Genoese in Galatea, at the same time urging his government to lose no time in taking advantage of the favourable circumstances. In the event neither Venice nor Dushan was in a position to take advantage of the situation in Constantinople. External circumstances were unfavourable and neither had the strength for such an undertaking. It is likely that Dushan was aware of the Serbian party in the capital and some discussions may have taken place. Nevertheless after the Battle of Maritsa there is no evidence of any move by him against the capital. His decision not to act was not due solely to weakness; other factors, particularly the threat from Hungary, held him back.

Relations with Bulgaria

In the 13th century the Bulgarian Empire played a leading role in the Balkans but with the rise of Serbian power on the eve of Dushan's accession, Bulgaria was fatally weakened by the defeat inflicted by Serbia at the Battle of Velbudz. At the accession of Dushan both states were in friendly relations, sometimes acting in concert but in any case not interfering with one another. The Bulgarian Emperor maintained his independence and succeeded in extending the boundaries of his state.

The basic factor in the relationship between the two states was the close family links between the two rulers. Dushan was married to the sister of Alexander of Bulgaria. This marriage had important consequences not only for Bulgaria but also for the internal situation in Serbia. Florinski has concluded that both Helen, the wife of Dushan, and Alexander were of Serbian stock from the family of Caesar Voihn, and were raised and educated in Serbia. This would seem to be confirmed by the fact that the relatives of Helen played an important part in Serbia at this period, being among the leading men in the State, e.g. Oliver, Deyan and Bogden to whom Dushan, in accordance with the Byzantine custom, granted the titles of despot, sebastocrat and caesar. The younger sister of Helen, Theodora, was married to the despot Uglesh Mernyachevich, one of the most powerful men in Serbia. Alexander, as a relative of the murdered Bulgarian Tsar Michael, was one of a number of Serbians sent by Decanski to support Nedi and her young son on the throne. In 1331 a revolution established Alexander as ruler and Nedi and her son were forced to leave Bulgaria. The events in Bulgaria coincided with the revolution in Serbia which put Dushan on the throne.

The wedding of Dushan took place very soon after his accession, in September 1331, and in 1332 ambassadors from Dubrovnik congratulated the rulers of Serbia and Bulgaria on the occasion of their entering into close family relationship. 'Not much time passed before the new King of Rascie (Serbia) took in matrimony the sister of Alexander the Emperor of Bulgaria.' There was probably a close link between those events; the revolt of Dushan against his father and the movement against Decanski's sister and Shishman, lawful heir to the Bulgarian throne, were probably masterminded by one of the leaders of the great Serbo-Bulgarian families, the Grebostrekovich. Decanski had not given his consent to the marriage between Dushan and Helen and this was one of the pretexts for the disagreements between Dushan and his father. Conscious of the role they could play under Dushan, the Grebostrekovich may have incited Dushan to arrange the death of his father. At the same time Alexander, on the point of seizing power in Bulgaria, counted on the fact that Dushan, now ruler of Serbia, would willingly recognise the revolution in Bulgaria. This would be a reward by Dushan for the services the Grebostrekovich had performed for him in Serbia. In addition Dushan was likely to feel more sympathy for Alexander than for Shishman, since a friendly ruler would guarantee against attack from Bulgaria – though the Bulgarians could not easily forget the defeat of Velbudz – and this was vitally important for Dushan at a time when he was carrying out his own revolution in the period immediately following his seizure of power.

These circumstances, then, the close family links between the two rulers, influenced the character of their relations. Helen and her brother exercised strong influence on Dushan, not permitting him to entertain the prospect of increasing his power at the expense of the neighbouring state of Bulgaria. In fact Dushan gave Alexander complete freedom of action and Alexander, now calling himself John Alexander Asen, Emperor of the Bulgarians and Greeks, strongly resisted that subordination to which Bulgaria had been subjected by Milutin and Decanski.

The family relationship led the two rulers to act in concert in political affairs. Alexander as a usurper was haunted by the fate of Shishman. Knowing that the lawful ruler whom he had deposed, was living with his mother in Dubrovnik, Alexander turned to Dushan with a request to put pressure on the Republic to hand them over. Dushan tried to achieve this by negotiations but was prepared to use force if necessary. In return for this service Alexander was prepared, according to one source, to become a vassal of Dushan, 'con promessi di farli tributario'. This view cannot be accepted; Luccari, from whom Florinski quotes, seems to have regarded Alexander as some sort of governor of Bulgaria for Dushan, claiming that Alexander was upset at the 'coolness' of Dushan over the question of Shishman, and asked Dushan to give him an imperial crown! We are told that Dushan granted this request obliging Alexander to supply yearly 12 hunting dogs as a sign of vassalage to him as lawful ruler of Bulgaria. In time of war Alexander would be obliged to supply at his own expense 12,000 cavalry to aid Dushan. This account must be regarded as largely fictitious. Alexander was proclaimed Emperor in 1331 somewhat earlier or around the time Dushan was seizing the throne of Serbia. Consequently when Alexander made his request to Dushan regarding Shishman he was already Emperor. Indeed had he not been Emperor and independent ruler of Bulgaria there would have been no point in pursuing Shishman – that would have been the duty of Dushan as overlord.

Neither Cantacuzene nor Gregoras, who describe in detail the wars between Dushan and the Empire, make any reference to joint action of Serbia and Bulgaria. Italians, Germans, and Albanians are mentioned as auxiliaries of Dushan – not Bulgarians. Only on one occasion in the course of events recorded by Cantacuzene are the Bulgarians referred to as acting with the Serbians and that was at the Battle of Maritsa. Here, however, the Bulgarians were not acting as supporters of Dushan but as allies of John Palaeologus, taking a position different from that of Serbia, and their flight from the battlefield may indeed have contributed to the Serbian disaster.

Alexander was often at war with Byzantium, and like Dushan he intervened in the civil war but his actions must be seen as independent of Dushan, carried out for the benefit of Bulgaria not Serbia. One result of this was the acquisition of an important strip of land. Taking advantage of the weakness of the Empire, Alexander was acting not as the helper of Dushan but simply as his ally. He did not share the grandiose ambitions of his brother-in-law nor did he recognise any obligation to him.

In the first years of his rule Alexander, like Dushan, found himself at war with Byzantium. Taking advantage of the troubles in Bulgaria after the Battle of Velbuzd, Andronicus seized a number of cities from the Bulgarians; Alexander defeated the forces of the Emperor and was soon able to recover the cities. One of the conditions of the peace which followed was that the daughter of Andronicus should marry the son of Alexander, Michael Asen. But while peace was then signed between Bulgaria and Byzantium the relations between Byzantium and Serbia remained hostile until 1334. While arrangements for the marriage were in hand the relationship between Dushan and the Emperor had deteriorated and Dushan was carrying out military action in Albania. It is doubtful whether Alexander was concerned about the interests of Dushan, strengthened as he now was by the promised family alliance with Byzantium. Andronicus returned to his capital after a successful advance to the west, reuniting within the Empire the lost provinces of Epirus and Akarnin.

On the way to Adrianople he was met by Bulgarian emissaries who reminded him of the need to fulfil the promise given to Alexander regarding the marriage of his daughter to Michael Asen. According to Cantacuzene this was a promise that the Emperor would have preferred to forget; he wanted to keep his daughter at home rather than give her in marriage, for he knew that, educated in the Greek fashion, she would find life difficult among the 'barbarians'. Recognising, however, that the marriage would serve the interests of the State, he reluctantly gave his consent. The wedding in the presence of Alexander and Andronicus was celebrated at Adrianople. The bride and groom were still children; Michael and Maria were not more than ten. After the wedding ceremony the young couple returned to Bulgaria; many of the important Greeks accompanied Maria to Trnovo and a period of peace between Bulgaria and Byzantium followed. This was in marked contrast to the relations between Byzantium and Dushan. The forced marriage was an indication of just how dangerous Bulgaria could now be. This became evident on the death of Andronicus II when Cantacuzene proclaimed himself Emperor and began the period of civil strife within the Empire. In view of the family connection, Alexander was bound to favour the cause of John Palaeologus, but like Dushan the real object of intervention was to extend the frontiers of his own state. Cantacuzene had rejected a request to hand over Shishman who was now living in Constantinople. He was likely to be more successful with the young Emperor.

When at the outbreak of the civil war Dushan offered his protection to the Emperor, Alexander tried to frustrate it. Twice he had the opportunity to seize the important cities of Thrace – Adrianople and Dimitok – and twice he was prevented by the Turkish allies of Cantacuzene. In 1331, when the civil war had scarcely begun, Adrianople, remaining faithful to the lawful Emperor, called on Alexander for assistance against Cantacuzene. That same year, when Cantacuzene was a guest in Serbia, his wife Irene, held in Dimitok by the military action of the opposition party, called on Bulgaria for help. Alexander appeared, dismissed the leaders, then invested the city and tried to take it by force. In order to ensure success he sent an emissary to Dushan asking him not to release Cantacuzene but to have him killed, a request rejected by Dushan. It may safely be assumed that Dushan was not rejecting this request on moral grounds! There were a number of very good reasons why Dushan should prefer to see Cantacuzene alive. His death would leave Palaeologus in undisputed possession of the Empire dependent on Bulgarian support, as a reward for which the Bulgarians would gain Adrianople and Dimitok, which lay too close to the capital for comfort. Bulgarian emperors had successfully challenged Byzantium in the past. Dushan could not ignore the possibility that Alexander had plans of his own and might follow the example of Simeon and Samuel, making the Emperor little more than a puppet of Bulgaria. In the event Irene was rescued by Omar and his Turks who forced the Bulgarians to retreat.

In 1350 Cantacuzene, still Emperor, attempted to persuade Alexander to co-operate with him in the construction of a fleet for the defence of the coast against Turkish attacks. The real aim of the Emperor was quite different; he was not concerned with the safety of Thrace or the protection of Bulgaria from Turkish attack. The money and fleet which he was requesting from Alexander was not for the purpose of defence but against another enemy, since he feared an attack from the West. Bulgaria had suffered from the devastation of the Turks, nominally the allies of Cantacuzene, and the responsibility for this could with some justification be attributed to the Emperor. If these proposals were an attempt to lessen Bulgarian resentment they must be regarded as having failed. According to Cantacuzene, Alexander was ready to enter into alliance with him, but acting on the advice of Dushan did not give him the money to build a fleet. This is the only episode which could justify the claim that Alexander was not carrying out an independent policy, and does not necessarily imply dependence. The family relationship between the rulers in fact prevented the union of the two Slav states which seemed possible after the Battle of Velbuzd. Peace was maintained between them but each carried out his own policy, similar – but ultimately irreconcilable – only in the sense that the object was the weakening of the Byzantine Empire. The prize would ultimately go to the stronger and by interfering in Byzantine affairs Alexander indirectly furthered the growth of the Serbian state, but clearly this was not Alexander's intention.

It is doubtful in any case whether Alexander was in a position to provide help to Dushan. We know little of the internal situation in Bulgaria prior to Alexander's seizure of power, but what we do know does not argue in favour of Bulgarian strength. Alexander was a usurper; we have seen how concerned he was at the possibility of the restoration of Shishman. He owed his position to the support of the boyars and they were unreliable at the best of times. Alexander had, it is true, extended the boundaries of the State but the acquisition of territory had been achieved thanks to relatively favourable circumstances, in particular as a result of the unrest in the Byzantine Empire and not as a result of Bulgarian strength. In 1334 he was aided by the Tatars; Philipol and Rhodop were granted voluntarily by Byzantium. His own military efforts were not distinguished by success; he was unable to capture Adrianople and Dimitok, nor did he succeed in conquering Morea. He was not even in a position to defend his own territories against the Turks who devastated southern Bulgaria; though seriously concerned at these attacks his failure to take action suggests lack of means rather than lack of will. But Bulgaria also suffered from the other 'barbarians' the Tatars. The fact that Alexander had made use of the Tatars did not preserve the country from their plundering. In addition to these external threats Bulgaria was still plagued by the problem of the Bogomils, the dualist sect which flourished in spite of the condemnation by the Council of Trnovo (1211). The difficulty of crushing this heresy came from its versatility and its ability to adapt to circumstances. The Bogomils never scrupled to ally themselves with other religious and secular groups and were therefore difficult to detect. Internal problems, therefore, and the lack of military power, which in any case was essential for the defence of his own territories, meant that Alexander was not in a position to help Dushan. But it is not certain that Dushan himself was anxious to maintain close relations with Bulgaria; the family links of themselves did not necessarily imply understanding and trust. Alexander's attempt to incorporate Adrianople and Dimitok into his empire can hardly have been pleasing to Dushan. Alexander, like Dushan, had his sights fixed on Constantinople.

In 1349 Dushan concluded peace with Dubrovnik, resolving the question of free trade in the Serbian Empire, with the proviso that such freedom of trade – particularly that of arms – should not be to the advantage of Serbia's neighbours and potential enemies, including Bulgaria 'neither in Bulgaria nor Bessarabia nor Hungary nor Greece'. In 1352 when Dushan had failed to obtain an alliance with Venice, Alexander established friendly relations with the Republic, promising them unrestricted trade in the Bulgarian

Empire and all support and protection. Anyone opposing them would be regarded as traitors 'sia traditore del mio imperio'. It is probable that the Venetians were more concerned to gain support in their struggles against the Genoese than to become involved in a conflict between the two Slav powers. The rivalry between Bulgaria and Serbia could only help the Turks above all and to a lesser extent the Western powers who were attempting to re-establish their domination over the Balkans. Byzantium had long ceased to be a threat.

Relations with Hungary and the Papacy

Although the Church in Serbia was Orthodox, the conquests of Dushan resulted in the inclusion within the Serbian Empire of areas in Dalmatia predominantly Catholic. This was bound to involve Dushan in relations with the Papacy. Neighbouring states, Bosnia and Hercegovina, were under Western influence, Croatia, now virtually an appendage of Hungary, was Catholic, and Hungary was the main enemy of Serbia on political and religious grounds, so that a Hungarian attack on Dushan could be justified on grounds of 'heresy'. In fact the King of Hungary considered himself as king of the purely Serbian lands lying east of Bosnia on the right bank of the Danube. His aim was to establish Hungary as the dominant power in the eastern Balkans, justifying his claim as a faithful son of the Catholic Church and relying on the support of the Pope. Hungarian aggression against Serbia could be hidden under the cloak of religious respectability as a Crusade against a 'schismatic'. In 1308 Charles Robert, a representative of the Angevin dynasty ruling in southern Italy ascended the throne of Hungary, and dreamed of restoring the Latin Empire in Constantinople, the titular head of which was Philip of Tarento. The accession of Charles Robert opened the possibility of united action between Hungary, Poland and Naples. Louis who succeeded his father in 1342 attempted to realise the grandiose plans of Charles Robert and indeed to go beyond them. His failure to win Naples was counter-balanced when, on the death of Casimir II he gained the throne of Poland, thus uniting in his person the two most powerful states in central Europe at that time; in addition he had plans to unite Bohemia under his rule by a marriage between his daughter and the son of the Czech King Charles IV. From this powerful base in central Europe he aimed to extend his power in the Balkans, particularly on the lower Danube. The restoration of the Dalmatian towns to Hungarian rule, war with the Tatars, Vlachs, Serbians and Bulgarians was an expression of that aim. The Pope, now an exile in Avignon, reminded Louis of his duty as defender of the true faith to root out heresy and schism in the East; in fighting Dushan he would be resisting the spread of heresy. Serious danger therefore threatened Serbia from the north.

Dushan was aware of the forces gathering against him in the north, which may explain his decision to concentrate on the south-east where he could expect easier and more lasting victories and make an attempt on Constantinople. He was less concerned with saving the western parts of the Serbian lands from attack from the West. His failure to tackle the danger from the north-east meant that the Slav lands in the west never became part of his empire; instead of concentrating his efforts on creating a compact and powerful Slav state he wasted his strength on an ultimately futile attempt to create a Slav-Greek Empire with himself replacing the Palaeologi in Constantinople.

In 1332 Charles Robert made preparations for an attack against the 'heretic schismatic' on his borders. The attack, however, took place only in 1334. Knowing that Dushan was involved in the conquest of Macedonia, Charles Robert 'with a great army' crossed the Danube into central Serbia believing, mistakenly, that the land was undefended. Dushan, however, had made peace with Andronicus at Salonika, having failed to capture the city despite the fact that some of the citizens had been ready to hand it over. Once peace had been concluded he advanced to meet the Hungarians. Charles then withdrew, possibly feeling the forces at his disposal to be insufficient to guarantee victory. The retreat was only partially successful, many troops being lost crossing the river. Cantacuzene attributes the retreat of the Hungarians to the help which Dushan obtained from Andronicus. Cantacuzene further claims that a cause of hostility between Dushan and Charles Robert arose over the control of Machva. Machva and Belgrade had long been a bone of contention between Serbia and Hungary. It will be remembered that Belgrade had been granted to Dragutin as a vassal of the Hungarian king, and was therefore considered as an integral part of the Hungarian kingdom. Danilo states that in the course of the war against Hungary Dushan invaded enemy territory on the Serbian border 'ide v'okrst'nye predel dr'zav svoje'. If this evidence can be accepted Serbian troops did not remain there for long; whether or not Serbian troops occupied these territories the city of Belgrade remained in Hungarian hands. Only towards the end of his reign in 1353 did Dushan make a last unsuccessful attempt to gain control of the right bank of the Danube.

After the unsuccessful action against Serbia in 1334, the attacks were not renewed. Charles Robert was too much involved over the question of Naples and Poland and in relations with the West. The Pope urged him to act against Serbia. After the accession of Louis attacks against Serbia became more frequent; Louis was even more fanatical in his aim of extirpating heresy than his father had been. Bosnia under the Ban Dominic Oslo was the means by which he hoped to achieve his aims. In the first 10 years of his reign Louis was not in a position, in view of his commitments in the West, to mount an attack against Serbia. His policy in Naples was opposed by Pope Clement VI. Thus in the first 10 years of his reign Dushan was in a position to act energetically in the western areas. In fact this did not happen and he entered into friendly relations with Louis, offering to mediate in the war between Hungary and Venice, an offer which was accepted by the Venetians. It is impossible to say whether Dushan's efforts were responsible for the ending of the war but peace was concluded. From the Serbian point of view this was a serious error of judgement. It was clear that once peace had been made with Venice, and a settlement reached over Naples, the King of Hungary would seek compensation in the east to make up for his defeat over Naples.

The growing power and expansion of Serbia was bound to bring it into conflict with Bosnia. As neighbours at a time when borders were not clearly defined, conflict was inevitable. Trebinje lay in the far north-western part of Serbia. Hum belonged to the Ban of Bosnia. Dushan continued to insist that Hum was purely Serbian; in correspondence with the Doge he described himself as 'Stephanus dei gratia Servie, Dioclea, Chilminiae (Hum) rex'. The peninsula of Punt and the town of Ston and areas surrounding it could be regarded as belonging equally to the Ban or Dushan. Because of the need for money these territories were in effect sold to Dubrovnik in return for a payment of 8,000 perpers, and an annual rent of 500 perpers (Venetian). But though peace was maintained at this period, the Ban was vassal of Louis of Hungary, and was bound to be involved if and when hostilities began between Dushan and Louis. The Ban carried out a series of attacks in the vicinity of Trebinje, capturing many Serbian subjects and 'facevano grave danno nel contadi di Trebine'. Dushan, fully occupied in attacking Byzantium, failed to take action against Bosnia. This lack of interest in the western areas of his State was not merely a consequence of his ambitions with regard to Byzantium, but also indicated his obsequiousness towards Venice. The Venetians were anxious to effect a reconciliation between Dushan and the Ban. They feared that the Ban was not seriously considering war and they did not wish to see him defeated or weakened. On the one hand they hoped to win him as an ally against Hungary; on the other hand they were uneasy at the prospect of Dushan attempting to annexe territory in their neighbourhood. They understood very well that all the Serbian lands under one powerful ruler could have serious consequences for them and the Latin states in the Balkans. Dushan never seems to have realised the threat he posed to Venice and was trying to enlist their support for a war against Bosnia. In 1346 he agreed to a proposal from the Venetians for reconciliation with the Ban subject to three conditions: first all territories seized illegally by the Ban should be returned unconditionally, failing which, secondly the disputed territories should be decided by a third party. Thirdly, if these conditions proved unacceptable to the Ban there should be a cessation of hostilities for two or three years.

It is not certain whether the Ban accepted any of these proposals; it may be that Dushan hoped for a refusal which would justify a continuation of hostilities against Bosnia. In any case hostilities were renewed in 1349. This date is confirmed by the fact that an ambassador was sent from Venice to Serbia with instructions to attempt another reconciliation between the belligerents. The attempt failed, however, for the reasons given by the ambassador. Dushan, he said, claimed that the Ban 'returned evil for good' and 'continued to seize Serbian lands and citizens'. Consequently Dushan would demand satisfaction from the Ban. Let the Doge use his influence to persuade the Ban to return the lands and citizens he had seized; otherwise he could delay no longer. The Senate tried to soothe Dushan, expressed sympathy and promised to induce the Ban to satisfy the Serbian claims. If such an attempt was made along these lines it obviously failed. The final rejection of a military alliance against the Byzantine Empire by the Venetians may have been a factor in deciding Dushan to concentrate his forces in the west. In July 1350 he began his preparations for war. Venetian plenipotentiaries at the courts of Dushan and the Ban had no success. When in September of the same year a second attempt was made by Venice, Dushan was probably already in action. His army crossed the River Drina into Bosnia. The timing of the advance was favourable; Louis of Hungary was involved in Italian affairs and was not in a position to defend 'his' territories. Ban Stephen prepared to meet the enemy but avoided pitched battles in the open field while strengthening the towns and mountain passes in the hope of delaying the advance of the Serbian army. The failure of this plan was due in part to the transfer of allegience of many of the boyars from the Ban to Dushan who advanced deep into Bosnia, capturing Hum which had to submit to his rule. The campaign was cut short, however, by the news that Cantacuzene and his Turkish allies were attacking Macedonia. The light forces which Dushan had at his disposal in Macedonia were no match for the Turks, who plundered and captured towns. In a series of forced marches he suddenly appeared before Salonika with an army which, though smaller, was stronger than that of the Greeks. It was here that a meeting took place between Dushan and Cantacuzene, when the latter was reminded how Dushan had welcomed him as a fugitive; now Cantacuzene was repaying him by seizing his territories. Dushan had one part of the Empire while Cantacuzene had the other half which he had taken from 'another' – a clear reference to the legitimate and sole ruler, John Palaeologus. Dushan's conditions for peace were to be based on the status quo – the frontiers as they existed before the war. Cantacuzene demanded the return of Epirus and Thessaly and the Macedonian Littoral, ceding the hinterland to Dushan. This is Cantacuzene's own account; it is difficult to know how accurate it is.

In the spring of 1351 Dushan returned to Bosnia, his aims being similar to those of the previous year – punishment for the Ban. At the same time the Venetian ambassador to Serbia was reminded of the danger to the defenceless Dubrovnik if Serbia mounted an attack. Dushan was not prepared, however, to encroach on the freedom of Dubrovnik or any other Venetian possessions. Nevertheless the Venetians were anxious to bring hostilities between Serbia and Bosnia to an end. Dushan's conditions for peace were that the daughter of the Ban should marry his son Urosh, Hum to be given as a dowry. This proposal was unacceptable to the Ban since his daughter was already promised to Louis of Hungary. Consequently negotiations broke down. Dushan's real aim was the ultimate union of Bosnia and Hum with the Serbian Empire; if it could be achieved by marriage that was preferable to war. Failing to achieve his aims in Bosnia he returned to Serbia, visiting Dubrovnik on the way. Though the Serbian army was in effective control of Hum the Ban was not prepared to accept the loss of this territory and, irritated by the rejection of his marriage proposals, Dushan then turned his back on the west and no further plans were made to include Bosnia in the many titles he assumed. Hum, that is the Serbian Littoral from Dubrovnik to the River Tsetnje, was the sole gain.

Hungary remained the greatest threat to Dushan. With the settlement of the Neapolitan question Louis' hands were now freed for renewed action in the Balkans. To regain the territories lost by the Ban was his first obligation. He regarded Hum as part of the dowry of his wife Elizabeth. Dushan was not only an enemy of Hungary but in possession of territory 'rightly' belonging to him; added to this was his religious fanaticism which saw Dushan as the great schismatic. As a faithful son of the Catholic Church it was his duty to bring the Serbian ruler back to the true faith. The growth of Serbian power was seen as a threat to the Latin states in the Balkans; the conquest of Macedonia, the assumption of the imperial title, the annexation of Epirus, Thessaly, Etolia and Akernin, the unsuccessful war against Bosnia, all following in fairly quick succession, were alarming for those in the West who were directly concerned with the consolidation of their power in the peninsula. The Angevins were closely linked with Albania, the Venetians were worried about their rule in Dalmatia, the Dukes of Achiae and Athens feared an attack against their lands in Ellad and the Pelopennese. It was clear that Byzantium, whose territories they divided amongst themselves, and where they still hoped to recreate the Latin Empire, was no longer a serious threat.

Since Dushan called himself Emperor of the Serbians and Greeks, and was aiming to replace the Palaeologi in Constantinople, it was reasonable to assume that by capturing the lost territories of the Empire he could demand the imperial crown as the restorer of the Byzantine Empire. In view of his constant attempts to form an alliance with Venice against the Empire his plans were well known in the West. In addition Dushan regarded himself as Emperor of the 'pravoslav' (Orthodox Christians) and, unlike Stephen First Crowned, did not consider that he required the sanction of the Pope to carry out his political plans. In spite of his close relations with Venice he maintained his antipathy to the West and only once, at a critical period for himself, was he prepared to compromise his religious principles. His attitude towards the Orthodox Church was an indication of his deep religious feelings, even if his donations to Greek monasteries were designed to win Greek support. The legal restrictions imposed on Catholics in his lands increased Western hostilities. In 1350 Pope Clement VI exhorted Louis of Hungary and the Doge to take steps to stop Dushan persecuting Catholics and forcibly turning them into 'heretics'.

War, allegedly in the interests of the Catholic Church, broke out between Hungary and Serbia in 1352. Dushan at first decided to resist, but in view of the apparent strength of the Hungarians he withdrew into the narrow valleys and Louis decided to try to achieve his aims by negotiations. At a meeting between the two rulers Louis laid down the conditions for peace: first the recognition of the Catholic Church and obedience to it. Secondly all lands belonging to the King of Hungary should be returned. Thirdly Dushan should recognise Louis as his overlord, and finally Dushan's son should be given as hostage. These conditions were quite unacceptable to Dushan. The very fact that Louis was ready to negotiate indicated that he lacked the strength to ensure victory over Dushan; these were the kind of terms a victor might have imposed and Louis was not a victor. Fighting therefore continued but the planned invasion of Serbia did not take place. The constant threat from Hungary led Dushan to enter into negotiations with the Pope who, in view of the expressed willingness of the Emperor for reconciliation with the Catholic Church, restrained Louis from carrying out his religious mission. The motives behind the change of attitude on the part of Dushan are not clear, and could hardly be reconciled with his position as defender of the Orthodox faith. It may be that the reverses he had suffered in the east, particularly at the hands of the Turks at Maritsa, had convinced him that he lacked the power for the time being to oppose the Hungarians. The defensive war he had conducted against Louis, and his decision not to face the enemy in open conflict, appear to indicate that the forces at his disposal were inadequate. For these reasons he attempted to turn to diplomacy and a rapprochement with the Pope, and proclaimed his willingness as a faithful son of the Catholic Church to carry out the orders of the Holy Father.

Since the pretext for the war against him was his heresy his submission to the Pope would remove any justification for a Hungarian attack. This volte face on his part must be regarded as a tactical move; he had no intention of abandoning the Orthodox faith. Indeed nothing could have been more likely to weaken his support among the Greeks whom he was trying to reconcile to his rule. The Emperor in Constantinople was traditionally the defender of the Orthodox faith, and since Dushan's ultimate aim was to gain the imperial crown for himself, a change of faith was the one thing calculated to prevent the realisation of that ambition. If, from a strictly moral point of view, Dushan's action can be condemned, it could be argued that Louis of Hungary was also using religion as a cloak for aggression. Dushan was not the first nor would he be the last Orthodox leader to seek Papal support to further his own ends. Nor is it likely that the Pope had any illusions regarding the sincerity of such a conversion. The immediate object was to halt the Hungarian attack.

In the summer of 1354 plenipotentaries were sent to Avignon. Venice, with which relations were friendly at that point, recommended the Serbian ambassadors to the Pope. In the name of the Emperor these ambassadors recognised the supremacy of the Papacy and promised full religious freedom to Catholics in Serbia. Forced conversion to the Orthodox faith would be prohibited, and Catholic churches seized would be restored. Dushan expressed his willingness to accept all the conditions of the Pope. All this was done for the sake of appearance; Dushan went to the length of suggesting the appointment of himself as leader of a Christian Crusade against the Turks. In fact there is no evidence that Dushan was greatly concerned with the Turkish danger, the full extent of which he, along with the other rulers in the Balkans, failed to grasp. Receiving the blessing of the Pope for a war against the Turks ensured his territories against an attack from Hungary. The Pope was delighted with these signs of submission, thanked Dushan for all he had done, wished him a long and happy reign with success in war, and was glad to name him as captain for the fight against the Turks. A Papal mission was sent to Serbia via Hungary requesting the Hungarian king to provide aid to the legates in their mission to Serbia undertaken for the unification of the Church. It may be assumed that the Pope was making a plea to Louis to maintain peaceful relations with Dushan.

Innocent was no doubt conscious of the fact that the conversion of the Serbian people could not be carried out by the Emperor alone, and attempts were made to influence the leading men in the State. To the Patriarch Ioannik the Pope wrote reminding him that he was exercising his high office illegally 'quamquam illicite' and must follow the way of truth; messages of a similar kind were sent to all archbishops and bishops, and to all leading personalities in government. Innocent failed to realise the kind of man he was dealing with; there was never the slightest possibility that Dushan would abandon the faith of the Greeks and the Slavs. An interesting account of the negotiations between the Papal legates and the Emperor is given in the life of Bishop Peter by Philip de Mezieres, which also throws an interesting light on the ritual of the Serbian court. The Emperor received the legates haughtily 'superbe nuncium papalem recepit'. Peter then disclosed the object of his visit, but the attitude of the Emperor was so hostile that Peter believed himself in danger of death. Negotiations continued for some days and followed a similar pattern; agreement would be reached only to be rejected at the next meeting. Finally, according to this account, the Emperor raised many objections and began openly to express his ill-will towards the Catholic Church, issuing a decree forbidding Catholics to attend Mass under pain of blindness. Peter, however, declared his intention to hold Mass despite this threat, 'hourly expecting death'. Among those attending Mass were some 300 Germans, probably miners. Thereupon, according to Peter, the Emperor summoned the Germans who had defied his orders, knowing the penalties for such disobedience, to which they replied that they feared God more than they feared him, adding that the Emperor knew they were Catholics and members of the Roman Church. If the Emperor was determined to punish them 'they were ready not only to sacrifice their eyes but their lives in defence of the Catholic faith'. This so astonished the Emperor that his attitude changed, nevertheless he continued in his 'heresy'. Peter did succeed in obtaining the restoration of many Catholic churches.

Clearly the negotiations with the Pope had never been seriously intended to lead to conversion but simply to gain time; from that point of view they were successful. Louis, fulfilling his promise to the Pope, left Serbia in peace and went off to fight the Tatars and aid the Polish King Casimir in the conquest of Galicia and the Ukraine. At the same time Dushan found an ally against Hungary. In 1355 a marriage was arranged between Urosh and Elena, the daughter of the Vlach Prince Vlaska, whose independence was threatened by Hungary. The union enabled both rulers to take joint action against the common enemy. A second alliance was formed with Venice, similarly threatened by Hungary in Dalmatia. In the middle of 1355 there were rumours of a Hungarian movement towards the Adriatic. A war between the Catholic states would, Dushan believed, enable him to strengthen his position in the west. But as an ally of Venice he damaged his own interests and those of the Slavs in general. His sister Elena had married the Croat Prince Mladin, ruler of the cities of Klios and Skradin. On the death of her husband Elena entered into negotiations with her brother to hand over these cities to him, which were then occupied by Serbian garrisons. The possession of these strategically important cities opened up the way for an advance into Dalmatia and a chance to fight Hungary. However, Dushan not only failed to take advantage of his opportunity but was unable to hold the cities themselves. Klios was besieged by the Ban of Croatia acting on behalf of the King of Hungary. Skradin, in view of the difficulty of retaining it, was sold to the Venetians. Before this transaction was completed Dushan was dead.

CHAPTER IV

Urosh and the Fall of the Empire

THE EMPIRE THAT DUSHAN had created did not long survive him; in consequence his son and successor has been unfavourably compared with his father, the decline and final collapse of the Empire being attributed to his deficiencies as a ruler. But the collapse of the Empire, or perhaps more correctly the collapse of central power, did not follow immediately after the death of Dushan; the basic internal weaknesses which contributed to the fall of the Empire were present during the lifetime of Dushan, and had he lived he would have been forced to deal with them and might have been no more successful than his son.

According to Cantacuzene trouble broke out on the death of Dushan as a result of the attempt of his half brother Simeon to gain control of all the Serbian lands. But Cantacuzene is not a reliable witness. Greek narrative sources are concerned with southern Greek areas of the Serbian Empire, those most recently lost, but naturally not renounced by the Byzantine Empire, and they tended to equate conditions in these areas with conditions in the rest of the Serbian Empire.

The events which led to the destruction of the Empire began with an attack from outside. The first threat came from the Despot Nicephorus II Orsen who, immediately after the death of Dushan advanced into the southern part of the Empire; the death of Caesar Preljub, Regent of Thessaly, following almost immediately on the death of Dushan, deprived the frontier areas of an energetic leader capable of defending them. Nicephorus advanced into Thessaly and banished the wife of Preljub who had governed the areas after his death. Simeon suffered a similar fate in the southern part of Epirus where he had been regent when Nicephorus seized it. Thus very soon after the death of Dushan these areas ceased to be part of the Serbian Empire. Greek authority was speedily restored, but not the authority of the Emperor in Constantinople, since Nicephorus proclaimed their independence. He extended his rule to Kephalinin and endeavoured to regulate his relations with Serbia, entering into negotiations with Simeon, his brother-in-law, and offering marriage to the sister of the Empress Helen. But his attempts to banish Albanians recently settled in these areas led to an Albanian uprising and his death in battle. Janina, the widow of Preljub, and Simeon were victims of the aggressive policy of Nicephorus. Janina was compensated by being granted lands which her late husband had held as *voivod*. Simeon, however, seized the city of Kostur, raised an army and adopted the imperial title; for a short period the title of Emperor was held by both Urosh and Simeon, and a struggle between them began. Simeon's assumption of the imperial title followed only after his banishment from the territories he had ruled as regent. The internal disorders followed only after the seizure of Thessaly and Epirus by Nicephorus; it was the unfortunate combination of Dushan's death followed by that of Preljub, and the fact that Serbian rule was not firmly established in these areas, rather than internal disorders and the alleged weakness of Urosh's rule, that made the conquests of Nicephorus relatively easy.

The theory according to which Dushan had considered Simeon as possible successor cannot be accepted. In 1342, it is true, at a time when he was ill, and his son too young to rule effectively, Dushan had discussed the question of succession. Simeon is mentioned but only after Urosh, and from 1345 Urosh was the young King. In the following year when Dushan assumed the title of Emperor, Urosh was crowned as King, a clear indication of Urosh's right to succeed his father. Under this system of dual rule the Emperor ruled the 'Greek lands' while the King was granted the lands of Serbia, territories incomparably greater than those ruled by his predecessors. In view of the youth of Urosh the division was not of practical importance, but Urosh was undoubtedly the sole legitimate successor. Simeon was given the title of Despot and control of sensitive border areas, but the title of King was superior to that of Despot. Another theory according to which Simeon aimed to become joint ruler with Urosh is equally unacceptable; the joint ruler as we have seen bore the title of King. Since Simeon had proclaimed himself as Emperor – not joint Emperor – he was clearly aiming to replace Urosh as ruler over the whole of the Serbian Empire. Nor can the possibility be accepted that Simeon wished to be Emperor only of the 'Greek lands', since his assumption of the imperial title followed only after the greater part of these lands had been lost. He made no attempt before the death of Nicephorus to regain the Greek lands, but confined his attacks to the Serbian territories. From his capital of Kostur he advanced to the north 'to seize the patrimony and government of his brother Stephen' on the grounds that he had a just claim to these territories.

The assumption of the imperial title was regarded by Urosh and the greater part of the Serbian nobility as an act of usurpation, leaving Urosh no option but to defend his crown. It is doubtful whether many nobles supported Simeon – they had their own plans to carve out independent kingdoms which might have been frustrated if Simeon had been successful. The Empress Helen, now ruling Serres, was behind her son. Only John Comnenos Asen maintained friendly relations with Simeon. Nevertheless Simeon was able to amass an army of some four to five thousand men – a considerable force for that period – and attacked the provinces of Skadar and Zeta. There is evidence from Dubrovnik sources that he attempted to negotiate with Urosh, but it is not clear from his correspondence whether he was asking Dubrovnik to mediate between him and Urosh or whether he was trying to obtain an alliance with the Republic. The policy of Dubrovnik was to ensure the continuation of trade with Serbia; war would threaten that trade and should be avoided if at all possible. The Council expressed its willingness to negotiate but their efforts appear to have been fruitless for in 1358 Simeon was again attacking Skadar. His defeat finally dashed any hopes of seizing the throne from Urosh. On the death of Nicephorus he took over Thessaly and Epirus, founding a state finally separate from the Serbian Empire. On the other hand if Simeon regarded himself as Serbian Emperor, these lands would not be lost but restored. Already prior to the loss of these lands John Comnenos with the support of Venice had seized the areas of Kanina, Valona and perhaps Berat, virtually creating an independent state. His ambitions had become apparent even during the lifetime of Dushan. The Venetians established friendly relations with Asen, granting him Venetian citizenship in 1353, indicating the importance which Venice attached to the coastal areas and harbours which the Despot ruled as regent of the Emperor Dushan. Circumstances forced Asen to seek closer relations with Venice; the decision of the Venetians to back him was probably due to the threat from Hungary and to the fact that the Serbian state was still powerful. The result was to give Venice virtual control in these areas nominally ruled by Asen, against the will of Dushan but with the support of the Serbian court where the influence of the Empress Helen was strong. Even during the lifetime of Dushan, Asen had acted independently towards the central government; the Venetians called him 'Despot of Romania' or 'Despot of Avalon'. The relations between Asen and Simeon were close, linked by family ties and the common threat from Nicephorus. But if Asen depended on anyone it was the Republic of St. Mark. Virtually independent of the central government, strongly linked with Venice, loyal to Simeon, but without direct contact with Helen in Serres, nevertheless Asen failed to achieve complete independence as a ruler. He acted more independently during the lifetime of Dushan than in the years following the death of the Emperor.

It was clear that the death of Dushan would be followed by an attempt by Byzantium to regain the lost lands. Yet the territories of Serres, lying nearest to the Empire, were not the object of attack, priority being given to the Greek lands in the southern part of Dushan's empire. These attacks were the work of powerful Byzantine nobles for their own ends, linked neither with the Emperor nor with each other. Nicephorus and Matija Cantacuzene, brother and son-in-law of the former Emperor John Cantacuzene, did not attack simultaneously. As soon as Nicephorus had seized Thessaly and Epirus, separate attacks were carried out by John and Alexis Palaeologus and Matija Cantacuzene. The territories captured by the brothers became in practice states independent of Constantinople. These territories had never been securely controlled even under Dushan, an additional complication being the fact that some of them had been captured by pirates, and it is doubtful for instance whether the town of Christopol was captured from Serbia or from a pirate named Alexis – a further confirmation that the weakness of the central government did not begin after the death of Dushan.

The advance of Matija towards Serres was halted by his complete defeat. According to Cantacuzene he had entered into negotiations with the Arnont of Serres and the commander of Dram, Caesar Vojihon, in eastern Macedonia. But the failure to make contact with either of them and the troops sent by Urosh to help his mother, led to the defeat and capture of Matija who was then handed over to his enemy John Palaeologus. Either Matija had been misinformed about the internal situation in south-east Macedonia or the government was more stable than he had imagined. Serres was ruled by the Empress Helen after the death of Dushan, but not as supreme ruler, because for many years the authority of the Emperor was recognised. Although she became a nun and adopted the name of Elizabeth, Helen was formally recognised as ruler of Serres, but the principality was not in her time separate from the Serbian Empire. But Urosh had no actual control there and gradually formal mention of his name was abandoned. The friendly relations existing between Urosh and his mother do not suggest that Helen was attempting to create an independent state of Serres, and the fact of Urosh sending troops against Matija Cantacuzene is an indication not merely of a desire to help his mother but of the need to defend his territories. Not until the beginning of the 1360s is there evidence of Serres under independent rule.

While the death of Dushan sparked off the Byzantine attacks in the south, the attacks in the north from Hungary were inspired by conflict within the Serbian Empire. The Hungarian attack had been long planned but the internal struggle of two nobles of the family of Rastislalici with Urosh, and their appeal to the King of Hungary provided a pretext for a

Hungarian attack. The failure of Urosh to reconcile the weaker of the two, who held possessions on the banks of the Danube, led him secretly to cross the river and seek help from a Hungarian noble in return for a promise to embrace the Catholic faith. Despite his failure to reconcile the warring lords in the north and the fact that he was still engaged in hostilities with Simeon, Urosh was bound to resist the Hungarian king. Although the Hungarians were successful in the open field, the Serbian army retreated into the thickly wooded mountains where the Hungarians were unwilling to risk a battle and they recrossed the Danube in 1359. Nevertheless the Rastislalici remained vassals of the Hungarian king and their lands of Branichev were separated from the Serbian Empire. A further indication of the declining power of the central government was the attempt of one Zarko to establish a state in Zeta, which was under the control of Helen. Zarko was unsuccessful, however, and the Venetians considered him simply as 'Baron of the King of Ras'.

In this period which is characterised by the struggle for the succession and the external threat, there were still no territories where the feudal lords could be said to be ruling independently. The regents who governed the border areas, who might have been the first to take advantage of the alleged weakness of the central government after the death of Dushan, failed to establish autonomous states. The Regent Preljub died shortly after Dushan and almost simultaneously Simeon was driven from his lands by Nicephorus. The territories of Asen were separated from the Empire but there the influence of Venice was strong. While it is true that in the first five years of Urosh's reign the greater part of the border lands was lost, the central government was not threatened, the danger coming from abroad in the first place. Moreover the description of Urosh as a 'roi faineant' does not correspond with the facts; he intervened actively against Simeon to preserve his inheritance and sent help to his mother when Serres was threatened. The contrast with Dushan is unfair; Dushan had probably reached the limit of his power by 1355 and could only have declined. The consolidation of the heterogenous territories of the Empire was a more complex task than their conquest had been, made easier as it had been by the civil wars in Byzantium. Urosh guaranteed the trading rights of Dubrovnik and Venice, binding himself to pay for any damage suffered by the merchants, and there is no evidence of any decline in economic activity, usually one of the first things to suffer in periods of internal unrest. It was customary for Dubrovnik to send emissaries on the accession of a new ruler and to confirm their trading privileges. The failure to do so on the accession of Urosh is attributed by Jirecek to the fact that Urosh was involved in the war between Hungary and Venice as an ally of the latter, and to the internal disorder in Serbia. This disorder, however, relates to a later period.

The reign of Urosh was nevertheless characterised by the struggles of the nobles among themselves for power and influence. The most important of these were the families of Vojhinovic, Balshici and Mrnjavchevich. Voislav Vojhinovic was Regent of Konaval, Trebinje and Drina, to which Urosh added the territory of Hum. When the Hungarian army advanced into Serbia, Voislav demanded from Dubrovnik the area of Ston on the grounds that it was an integral part of Hum and belonged to him as ruler of that territory. The refusal of Dubrovnik to accede to this request led to war between Dubrovnik and Serbia. Peace was concluded in 1359 and Dubrovnik agreed to pay the sum of 4,000 perpers to Urosh. In 1360 Urosh confirmed the privileges of the Dubrovnik merchants, but when Louis of Hungary was preparing to attack Serbia, Voislav renewed hostilities against Dubrovnik this time allied with Kotor, 1361. Urosh ordered the arrest of all merchants from Dubrovnik within his territories; Dubrovnik retaliated by arresting all traders from Kotor and Prizren. The Great Council went so far as to offer a reward for Voislav! Peace was concluded in 1362. While technically this was a war between Serbia and Dubrovnik, in fact it arose as a result of a quarrel between the Republic and Voislav with Urosh acting as mediator.

As the power of Urosh declined that of the great men increased, no longer content to act as regents, but bent on carving out independent principalities for themselves. Voislav, the first and most powerful of them, was closely linked with Venice where he was granted citizenship before he died in 1363. Another such was Vukashin, Zupan of Prilep in the reign of Dushan and raised to the rank of Despot by Urosh. The second brother of the Mrnjavchevich family, Uglesh, was regent of the areas near Dubrovnik in the time of Dushan. Great changes also took place in Zeta, where the ruler Zarka, to whom the Venetians had granted citizenship, was replaced by the three brothers Balshici: Stratsimir, George and Balsha. In a charter Urosh granted freedom of transport through these territories and those of Voislav, the most important route to the interior passing through these lands. The establishing of the power of the Balshici family was probably linked with the wars against Dubrovnik; Bar, Budva and possibly Skadar were in their possession. In the second war with Dubrovnik and her neighbours the Balshici were allied with the Republic against Kotor and Voislav who sought Budva for himself. The Balshici achieved the odd distinction of being made citizens of both Venice and Dubrovnik (1361-2). The war between them and Voislav continued after the conclusion of peace with Dubrovnik. When Voislav attempted to borrow a galley from Venice his request was rejected on the grounds that he and his opponent were both subjects to the same ruler.

South of the areas ruled by the Balshici the lands were still designated 'zemlji tsara Sklavonije', the lands of the Emperor. In the neighbourhood of

Drac the most powerful personality was the Albanian Carlo Topija who began to style himself 'Prince of Albania'. An enemy of the Balshici, he at one time captured George; peace was concluded between them through the mediation of Dubrovnik but they were again at war in 1368. The last surviving charter of Urosh is dated 1356 in which he granted to the sons of Branka the monastery of Hilander.

The Turks meanwhile were extending their power from Gallipoli. When in 1362 Ohran died he was succeeded not by his son Halil, the son-in-law of John Palaeologus, but by Murad the founder of the Ottoman Empire in Europe. During those years when the Black Death was ravaging Europe, the Turks captured the remaining towns in Thrace. The rest of the Byzantine Empire began to lose its links with the Christian states. The Patriarch Kallistos was sent to Urosh, then in Serres, to conclude peace and negotiate an alliance against the common enemy. The death of the Patriarch prevented a meeting with the Emperor and his mother. No attempt was made to negotiate with Bulgaria with whom the Emperor was still at war over the claim to certain towns on the Bulgarian coast. In any case the internal situation in Bulgaria rendered such an alliance impossible. The Tsar Alexander, having shut his wife up in a monastery, excluded the son of the first marriage from the succession (John Stratsimir) in favour of the son of his second marriage, John Shishman. The King of Hungary took advantage of the situation to seize Vidin, capturing Stratsimir and keeping him in captivity for four years.

We do not know to what extent the changes in the neighbouring state of Bulgaria affected the situation in Serbia. Perhaps the crisis there over the succession made it imperative to ensure that a similar situation did not arise in Serbia. There appears to have been a feeling that Urosh, having no children, should have a joint ruler. The man chosen for the position was Vukashin Mrnjavchevich, a powerful figure in his own right, whose rule extended in all areas which were at least nominally under the control of Urosh. But he did not, as was the custom in Byzantium, bear the title of Emperor, nor that of autocrat as did the Serbian kings – which was later to be borne by his brother Uglesh and Lazar – but was simply known as King. The territories which Vukashin ruled were greater than those ruled by Urosh during the period when he occupied the position now held by Vukashin. Then Dushan ruled over the whole empire while Urosh ruled only the Serbian lands which limited him to the northern territories. Vukashin considered himself as ruler of the whole Serbian state. The lands he held in his own right lay on both sides of the River Shar with the cities of Prizren, Skopje and Prilep. As the first Serbian ruler who did not come from the Nemanje dynasty, Vukashin was regarded as a usurper by the Serbian nobles; more as a dangerous rival and powerful restorer of the central government than as king, he aroused suspicion and fear.

The career of Uglesh is linked with the principality of Serres which after the death of Dushan was governed by his widow Helen even for some years after she had taken the veil. This territory was not separated from the Serbian state; the rights of Urosh were recognised if only formally. All the evidence we have shows Helen to have been a capable and energetic ruler very far from being a mere figurehead. In fact Uglesh was virtual joint ruler with Helen. She was still ruling in 1365 but so far as the Byzantine Empire was concerned in 1366 Serres had a new ruler. The position of Uglesh was bound up with that of his brother Vukashin. From 1361 Vukashin was the most powerful personality at the Serbian court, regarded as equal with Urosh. Vukashin had gained his title in a perfectly legal way from Urosh because there was no other way in which he could have acquired it; there was no usurpation, Vukashin enjoyed all the rights and privileges of monarchy. Both Emperor and King sent ambassadors for instance to Dubrovnik over the question of taxation due to Serbia; both appear in paintings in various churches; both minted money. As soon as Vukashin became King his brother was granted the title of Despot, receiving this from Urosh and not from his brother.

As king and joint ruler with Urosh, the power of Vukashin was not limited to his own hereditary lands in Macedonia, but extended to all lands nominally ruled by Urosh. By 1358 Uglesh was playing a leading role in the government of Serres. He had married the daughter of Caesar Vojihne, one of the most powerful men in the area after the death of Dushan, as a result of which he became master of all the lands 'ch'ere a confini di Romania'. Nothing is known of Vojihne after 1357 and it is very likely that his lands fell to Uglesh. In practice from 1360 Helen had ceased to rule, but five years were to pass before she yielded power to Uglesh with the agreement of Urosh. The power of Urosh was weakening along with that of the Empress – the ability of Helen to maintain her rule in Serres ultimately depended on the power of Urosh – while that of Vukashin and his brother was increasing. Vukashin styled himself as 'kraljevstvo mi' my majesty, after the fashion of Dushan, while Uglesh was 'despotavo mi'; in later charters Uglesh styled himself as ruler of Serres, 'tsartsvo mi' or again as autocrat, which meant independent ruler, a title adopted by all Serbian monarchs beginning with Stephen First Crowned.

Vukashin strengthened his rule in the western part of Macedonia over territories stretching from Prizren to Kostor and from the Vardar to the Albanian mountains. The main cities were Prizren, Skopje and Ohrid; he did not have a fixed capital and moved from Prilep to Skopje and Brod. He minted his own money, at first bearing the heads of Urosh and himself, later with only his own head. He confirmed the trading rights and privileges granted originally by Dushan to Dubrovnik. Family links with the Balshici strengthened his position, and in alliance with George Balshici he was preparing an attack on Nicola Altomanovich, the nephew of Voislav. He was diverted from this by an appeal from his brother who was facing an attack by the Turks. Uglesh was attempting to form a coalition with other states threatened by the Turks, particularly Byzantium, offering money to the Emperor, and proposing reconciliation with the Church at Constantinople with which Serbia had been in schism since the creation of an independent Serbian Patriarchate in the reign of Dushan. At the Battle of Maritsa both Vukashin and Uglesh were killed. The Battle of Maritsa sealed the fate of Serres which ceased to exist as a principality after 1371 but did not immediately fall under Turkish rule, though the Turks extended their rule in the territories of Uglesh in western Thrace. The territories of Chalkidik were seized by the Byzantine despot, later Emperor Manuel, while the lands between Strum and the Vardar fell to the Dragash brothers. Once more south-east Macedonia was restored to Byzantium, but although the Emperor had regained the lands of which the Empire had been deprived by the conquests of Dushan, he was a Turkish vassal.

When news of the battle first reached the West it was believed that the Turks had been defeated. The Venetians indeed feared a Turkish-Byzantine alliance and were prepared to take steps against it. When the truth finally became known Pope Gregory XI informed the Hungarians that the 'godless' Turks had seized the whole empire of 'Romania' and forced the Emperor to pay tribute. The relationship between the Emperor and the Turks was not an alliance of equals but of vassal and overlord. Maritsa ended the independence of Byzantium and Bulgaria; the Serbian defeat decided the fate of Serbia as well as the fate of its neighbours who had hoped to profit from it. Not only did Vukashin's son Marko become a vassal of the Sultan, so also did John and Constantin Dragash and the Bulgarian tsar. The significance of the defeat of Uglesh was clearly recognised by the Emperor Manuel II. Immediately after the death of Uglesh, because of the Turkish advance, it was decided to give half of the lands of Mount Athos and Salonika to the *proniar* as the only means of preventing them falling to the Turks – to be restored once the danger had passed. When Marko and the Dragash were forced to take part with the Sultan in an attack against the Vlach, both were killed and their lands fell under Turkish control.

The immediate beneficiaries of the Battle of Maritsa were first Lazar who seized Novo Brdo 'and many other places' and Nicola Altomanovich who seized the territories bordering his own lands, while the Balshici, despite, or perhaps because of their family links with Uglesh, took Prizren. Since these lands were potentially threatened by the Turks the Balshici found it expedient to accept the status of Turkish vassals. It is probable, although there is no direct evidence, that Vuk Brankovich and the brothers Dragash extended their territories, Vuk becoming master of Skopje by 1377 at the latest, while the Dragash extended their territories at the expense of Marko whose inheritance had shrunk considerably after 1371, being confined to a small area in western Macedonia, and he was in no position to defend even the lands he nominally ruled. Nicola Altomanovich, the nephew of Voislav, became involved in war with Dubrovnik – not as Jirecek claims over the non-payment of the so-called tax of St. Demetrius since the attack against Ston took place after the tax had been paid. The war arose out of the claim of Nicola, as heir to Voislav, to that part of Hum lying within the confines of Dubrovnik. The Republic hoped that the neighbours of Nicola, concerned at his growing power and aggressive intent, would combine against him. But the Battle of Maritsa, by eliminating Vukashin and Uglesh, had removed the most dangerous enemies of Nicola, and while the position of Dubrovnik deteriorated that of Nicola improved. Nevertheless in 1372 Nicola offered peace which was eagerly accepted by Dubrovnik and by the middle of the year relations had been restored.

In the division of the lands of Vukashin's sons Nicola had not received much. Yet after Maritsa he was the most powerful ruler in the territories of the former Serbian Empire. Like his uncle, Nicola held the coastal Zupas of Drachevic, Konavlje and Trebinje; within the confines of these Zupas were part of the 'lands of Hum'. Nicola effectively controlled the coast from Bok to Ston, excluding the narrow strip belonging to Dubrovnik. The Balshici scored an unexpected success against Nicola in the course of 1371 or 1372, seizing Prizren and becoming masters of Berat, Valona and Chimar. The younger Balshici had married the daughter of Asen, but in spite of their acquisitions the Balshici could not compare with the power of Nicola, whose lands were less divided and more easily defended than those of his enemies.

The short-lived and uneasy peace among the nobles at that period encouraged Nicola to prepare an advance to those parts of Hum not in his possession. Serbian rulers were not prepared to renounce territories belonging to Hum, either to Bosnia or Dubrovnik. The family of Vojinovich considered themselves as legitimate heirs to the lands of Hum, and Nicola was more successful in attempting to recover them than Voislav had been, even if the attempt was finally unsuccessful. It is not surprising therefore that Nicola entered into alliance with Venice and the Balshici against Dubrovnik. According to Orbini, in his history of the Serbian kingdom, the Venetians agreed with Nicola and the Balshici that they should seize Kotor and Dubrovnik by a land attack while the Venetians launched an attack by sea. In the event of success the Balshici would obtain

Kotor and Drac while Nicola would get Ston. Dubrovnik informed Louis of Hungary of the Venetian intentions and asked him to intervene. Nicola enjoyed strong support at the Hungarian court and in a previous war between himself and Dubrovnik, Hungary had not intervened. Nevertheless the ambitions of Nicola and the Balshici threatened the interests of Hungary; Louis was particularly concerned with the power of Venice in the Adriatic. He was therefore ready to sacrifice Nicola, the more so as he had found a loyal ally and vassal in the person of Lazar Chrebljanovich.

It is not surprising that Nicola should form an alliance with Venice and the Balshici; this was not merely in accord with the situation at the time, but with the long-term aim of regaining the lost lands from Dubrovnik. The coalition was not directed against the Ban Trvtko of Bosnia and Lazar who were allied at the same time. Nicola, however, clearly regarded Lazar as a threat to himself since he made an attempt to have him killed, and Lazar turned to the Hungarian king for help, promising in return money and homage. At the same time he entered into negotiations with Trvtko, himself the bitter enemy of Nicola. In consequence a combined Hungarian and Bosnian force joined with Lazar in an invasion of Nicola's territories, completely defeating Nicola who was captured and blinded, ending his days in 1374. His opponents seized his lands, each taking those parts adjoining their own territories, except for Trebinje, Konavalje and Drachevic, which were taken by the Balshici although they had taken no part in the fighting. The Hungarians, who had played a major part in the defeat of Nicola, appeared neither to have gained nor demanded territorial compensation; it may be that the King was satisfied with having obtained a new vassal in the person of Lazar. One other beneficiary of Nicola's defeat was Vuk Brankovich.

In the last quarter of the 14th century the northern areas of the Serbian state increased in importance; their strategic significance was a consequence of the new political constellation in the Balkans after the catastrophe of Maritsa and the fall of Vukashin and Uglesh. These territories contained not only rich mines but provided refuge for those fleeing from the Turkish advance in the south. Here the most powerful personality was Lazar, especially after the fall of Nicola. Up to the 1360s there is no mention of Lazar in contemporary diplomatic documents. Loyal to Urosh, he made no attempt to follow the example of other nobles who were attempting to carve out independent states for themselves. Nevertheless his influence at court was strong. The leaders of Dubrovnik, always conscious of where power lay and the need to establish contact with whoever possessed it, made a gift to Lazar on the occasion of peace being signed between Serbia and Dubrovnik at Onogorh, although Lazar was not directly involved in the peace negotiations.

In the course of the struggle with Nicola, Vuk Brankovich had fought with Lazar; Vuk had a common interest in supporting Lazar rather than Nicola, his immediate neighbour, whose ambitions threatened the security of Vuk's lands. It is likely they divided the lands of Nicola between them. Lazar was now one of the richest rulers in Serbia, controlling two of the most important areas, Novo Brdo and Rudnik. Yet his power must not be overrated. The price of his victory was submission to the King of Hungary and his advance to the north was halted for a certain time. An indication of the limit of his power is shown by the fact that when Trvtko proclaimed himself King of Serbia, Lazar made no protest. Trvtko justified his claim as legitimate successor to the Nemanje dynasty although there were Serbians who had stronger claims, among others the brothers Dragash. In any case Serbia had a ruler who had a better right to the title – Vukashin's son Marko. He and his brother were confined to a small area in the south-east and were incapable of action. Unless we are to assume that Lazar did not want the title for himself – and this is out of character with what we know of him – then his failure to challenge Trvtko must be attributed to the fact that he did not feel himself sufficiently strong at that point.

During the period following the defeat of Nicola, Lazar consolidated his position and rewarded those lesser nobles who were prepared to recognise him as their lord. By the end of the 1370s he had extended his territories in the north, having defeated Radich Brankovich Rastislalic. Prior to the death of Louis of Hungary he appeared on the Danube, whether as an independent ruler or as a vassal of the King of Hungary is not known. In 1378 Louis was preparing an attack against Serbia, perhaps fearing the growing power of Lazar, whom he had supported against Radich Brankovich. The relations between the King and Lazar in the last years of Louis' reign are not clear but in 1382 after the death of Louis, Lazar not only renounced his allegiance but attacked Belgrade and Golubats. In addition, along with Trvtko, he became involved in the dynastic quarrel in Hungary which followed the death of Louis. On the eve of Kosovo he became reconciled with the new King of Hungary, Sigismund, accepting all his feudal obligations. By the end of the 1370s he had established himself on the right bank of the Danube.

While Lazar was extending his power, his actions were copied by Vuk Brankovich. During the reign of Dushan the Brankovich brothers controlled only their inherited lands. The expansion of Vuk began only after the Battle of Maritsa. His position was strengthened by his marriage with Maria, the daughter of Lazar, and his power grew with that of his father-in-law. They shared common enemies and the death of Vukashin and Uglesh strengthened their position. Their ambitions did not conflict; Lazar was advancing north at the expense of Radich Brankovich and Hungary, while

Vuk's gains were made at the expense of the sons of Vukashin and the Balshici. While Lazar seized Kuchevo and Branichev, Vuk seized Skopje from the sons of Vukashin and Prizren from the Balshici.

Among the Serbian nobles George Balshici was the son-in-law of Lazar and the latter had close connections with rulers outside Serbia, with Bulgaria through the marriage of his daughter with Tsar Alexander, and with the Ban of Bosnia, thus securing his eastern and southern frontiers. In addition he won the support of the Church by his gifts to monasteries particularly Mount Athos. But only when he had defeated Radich Brankovich did he assert his claim as ruler of all the Serbian lands, joining the name Stephen, the name of all the Nemanje rulers, to his own. The territories he controlled, however, comprised less than a quarter of the former Serbian Empire; it is true that he extended his control over territories which had been in the possession of Serbia in the time of Dragutin, but at its greatest extent the State of Lazar did not include the former lands of Vukashin and Uglesh, the Balshici, the brothers Dragash and Vuk Brankovich. Two other crowned heads existed in the person of Vukashin's son and successor Marko, and Trvtko of Bosnia who had extended his power at the expense of Nicola Altomanovich, and the successors of Trvtko continued to style themselves Kings of Serbia. Nor was the title of Lazar recognised by the King of Hungary by whom he was simply named 'Prince of the kingdom of Ras'.

The Turks meanwhile were continuing their advance into the Serbian lands. In 1381 they suffered a defeat at the hands of Crep and Vitomir. Sultan Murad soon afterwards seized Nish and attacked Toplic but was defeated by Lazar at Plochnik in 1386. Two years later the Turks suffered another defeat at the hands of the Bosnians. But these were essentially skirmishes between Serbian and Turkish raiding parties, and led to the decision of the Sultan to prepare a massive attack against Serbia. Apart from troops from Asia Minor and the Balkans, troops were summoned from Turkish vassals from east and west. The army was led by the Sultan in person accompanied by his sons Jacob and Bajazid. Marching through the territories of Constantin Dejanovich, who was compelled to join the Sultan, Murad advanced to Kosovo in the territory of Vuk Brankovich. Lazar made diplomatic and military preparations, first attempting to ensure himself against an attack from Hungary, with whom he had severed his feudal obligations at the time of his struggle with Nicola Altomanovich. In support of the Angevin claimant to the throne of Hungary Lazar had captured Belgrade, though this has been disputed. Now in view of the Turkish threat he became reconciled with Hungary through the mediation of his son-in-law the Ban of Machva and accepted the feudal obligations due to the late King Louis. Trvtko, realising that the Turks were as much a threat to

Bosnia as to Serbia, offered military help, withdrawing his army from Dubrovnik for use in Serbia, where it was joined by a force from Croatia. Among the Serbian leaders who took part in the Battle of Kosovo was Vuk Brankovich in whose territory the fighting took place. With Lazar were his sons Stephen and Lazarovich. The Turkish claim that Bulgarians, Albanians, Vlachs, Hungarians, Germans and Czechs fought with Lazar belongs to the realm of fantasy.

The Battle of Kosovo and the death of Lazar sealed the fate of Serbia. News of the battle spread beyond Serbia. It was at first believed that the Turks had been defeated, and Trvtko wrote to Florence in those terms, and similar accounts were received in Venice and France, where the victory was celebrated in the cathedral of Notre Dame. Although the Sultan retreated after the battle, this was only for the purpose of consolidating his forces and he was in a position to take advantage of his victory whenever he wished. Serbia became a vassal state of the Sultan; the lands of Vuk Brankovich, vitally important for further Turkish advance, were under Turkish control. Skopje was captured and all important towns fell to the Turks.

After the death of Lazar his wife Militsa took over the reins of government on behalf of her young son Stephen Lazarevich. Bajazid offered to make them Turkish vassals, an offer which she had no option but to accept, in view of the situation on the northern frontiers now being threatened by the Hungarian king Sigismund who, continuing the policy of Louis, was attempting to assert his rule in Machva and ensure possession of northern Serbia. Militsa's acceptance of the Turkish offer was conditioned by the need to avert the threat, because Vuk Brankovich, in the hope of strengthening his position in Serbia, was relying on Sigismund and continued to oppose the Turks. Militsa therefore sent Serbian troops to the Sultan for use against Hungary. Thus the Serbians found themselves fighting the Hungarians as vassals of the Turks. The failure of Vuk to obtain help from Hungary forced him to submit to the Sultan and accept the status of vassal. With the capture of Trnovo from the Bulgarians the Turks were now in a favourable position to launch a campaign against the Hungarian vassal states on the Danube and Hungary itself. When Stephen Lazarevich came of age in 1392 and took control of the government in Serbia, his mother retired to a monastery.

The Hungarian victory over the Turks at Rovina in 1395 in which King Marko took part as a vassal of the Sultan and in which he lost his life, encouraged the West to support Sigismund; English, Germans and French were present when the Hungarian ruler met the armies of the Sultan at Nicopolje. The forces of the Christians, weakened by disagreement over the question of command, were no match for the well disciplined troops of Bajazid, aided by Serbian units under the command of Stephen Lazarevich.

The Sultan made use of the victory to consolidate his position in the areas he had already conquered. One of the victims of the defeat was Vuk Brankovich, a large part of whose lands were given to Stephen.

The peoples of the Balkans were saved from complete destruction thanks to the threats to the Turks in Asia Minor by the advance of Tamurlane. Stephen took part in the Battle of Angora in which Bajazid was defeated and captured, which was followed by a struggle for succession among his sons. The internal struggle within the Turkish Empire provided Stephen with the opportunity to renounce his allegiance to the Sultan. Immediately after the battle he withdrew his troops to Constantinople where he was welcomed by the Emperor and granted the title of Despot; from this period Serbia was styled as a despotate. The main rival of Stephen, George Brankovich, in an effort to strengthen his position in Serbia, supported Suleiman in the struggle for the succession and was imprisoned by Stephen, but having managed to escape joined Suleiman and attempted in conjunction with the latter to prevent the return of Stephen and his brother to Serbia, but his armies were defeated at Tripolje near Kosovo.

The discussions held at Gallipoli between representatives of Byzantium, Venice, Genoa and the knights of Rhodes, who all had interests in the Levant, assumed the relationship between Stephen and the Sultan to be one of overlord and vassal. Thus, not only could Stephen expect no help from these quarters, provided their interests were safeguarded they were not prepared to support him and might even prefer the Sultan. In view of the internal struggle he was now faced with over the claims of his brother Vuk, Stephen found it expedient to come to an agreement with Sigismund at the end of 1403. He was granted Machva and Belgrade in return for accepting the Hungarian king as overlord. This generosity on the part of Sigismund may be attributed to the serious internal situation in Hungary at that time. Stephen then made peace with Suleiman and Brankovich. The threat of a possible invasion by Tamurlane of the European provinces of the Turkish Empire made it imperative that Suleiman should not be threatened from the rear, and was probably one of the reasons for his willingness to make peace with Stephen. Dissension among his opponents made it possible for him to preserve his Balkan territories, but he was soon involved in a fight with his brothers Musa and Muhamed.

The internal quarrel which broke out in Serbia after the conclusion of peace with Suleiman and Brankovich arose from the claims of Stephen's brother Vuk to part of the latter's territories, and provided an opportunity for outsiders to intervene. Vuk was supported by Suleiman and a Turkish army invaded the country and advanced as far as Belgrade. As a result Stephen was compelled to cede to Vuk the southern part of Serbia which Vuk ruled as a vassal of the Sultan. As such he, along with Brankovich, became involved in the struggle between Suleiman and his brothers for control of the Turkish Empire. On the death of Suleiman, Musa became the sole ruler in European Turkey but was soon involved in a struggle with Muhamed. While Musa relied on the support of those who were prepared to take advantage of the fratricidal struggle to free themselves from feudalism, he was abandoned by the Balkan princes. Faced with the danger from Musa, Stephen drew closer to Sigismund and obtained from him possessions in Hungary and the mining districts in Srebrnits in Bosnia. Stephen became the leader of the movement against Musa, and gathered round him all those who, in face of the common danger from the Turks, were prepared to sink their differences. Musa reacted by invading Serbia, the army of Stephen was defeated, four fortified towns seized and the inhabitants captured or slain. Stephen appealed to Muhamed who returned to Europe where a combined force of Serbians and Hungarians awaited him, and destroyed the army of Musa in 1413. The victory of the central power in the Turkish Empire had been assured thanks to the support of the Christians. As a reward for his help Stephen was granted some lands in eastern Serbia. In view of the need to maintain friendly relations with the Sultan and his successor Stephen was obliged to renew his feudal obligations; this did give him 14 years of peace and the country the opportunity of achieving some kind of economic recovery.

After the death of the last of the Balshici – Balsha III – the territory of Zeta was seized by Stephen which led to war with Venice over the question of the coastal towns. As a result of the peace negotiations with the Venetians the latter maintained their hold over the cities of Skadar, Ljesh and Ultsinj. The territories of Stephen now extended from the Danube and the Sava to the littoral of Zeta in the west; in the east as far as Timok, south as far as Skopje in Montenegro. He was now at the height of his power. The absence of an heir to Stephen raised the problem of the succession which became more acute as a result of his illness, making him anxious to settle the question before he died. He summoned a Council and proclaimed as his heir his nephew George Brankovich. Relations were strengthened with Sigismund at Tati in 1426, confirming that George and his successors would become vassals of the Hungarian king, and he was granted Machva, Belgrade and Golubits. George succeeded to the title of Despot on the death of Stephen in 1427. The first years of his reign were critical. Murad, the new Sultan, celebrated his accession to the throne by invading the country in the same year; aided by forces from Dubrovnik the Serbians were able successfully to defend Novo Brdo, but the Turks captured Nish and established a garrison there as a prelude to an attack against Hungary.

Although George Brankovich was a vassal both to Sigismund and Murad, Serbia speedily recovered from the devastation caused by the war; a French traveller in 1431 remarked on the richness of the country. In view of the circumstances prevailing at the time, George could not hope to continue the policy of strengthening the State which Stephen had followed. The economic resources of the State were exploited by the merchants of Dubrovnik; the leading positions in the State were held by foreigners. George made an effort to strengthen his position by giving his daughter to the Sultan Murad; in 1435 he came to an agreement with Venice over the frontier question, and he and his family were granted Venetian citizenship. His failure to grasp that the main enemy of Serbia – as of all Balkan rulers – was the Turks, led him to dissipate his strength in a futile war against Bosnia at a time when the influence of the Turks was increasing in that state and the Beg of the Sanjak of Skopje was pillaging as far as Belgrade, when one after the other of the feudal rulers of Albania were being subjected to Turkish rule and Murad was winning victories in Epirus. Sigismund was fully informed of the extent of the Turkish power in Serbia, Bosnia and Zeta; Serbia became the battleground for the wars between Hungary and the Turks and suffered appallingly. When finally as a result of the Hungarian victory the Turks withdrew from Serbia the Despot was forced to make peace by renouncing Branichev.

The death of Sigismund in 1437 offered a favourable opportunity for a Turkish offensive against Hungary. Turkish armies advanced into Erdelj and Serbia, capturing the fortified towns with the ultimate object of seizing the whole of the despotate to ensure their rear prior to an all out attack against Hungary. The Hungarians were not in a position to aid Brankovich and in spite of a spirited defence Smederov was captured by the Turks and the despotate ceased to exist as an independent state, Smederov being given to the Beg of Skopje. Novo Brdo continued the struggle till 1441. The consequences of the defeat were catastrophic for Serbia; widespread devastation, the destruction of towns and the enslavement of much of the population. The Despot and his family found refuge in Hungary where a struggle for the succession had broken out. He attempted to gain the Hungarian crown for his son Lazar but without success. When the choice fell on Vladislav III he joined the party supporting the son of Albrecht, in consequence of which he was deprived of his lands in Hungary and went to Zeta to make plans for the recovery of the despotate. But all efforts to win support failed owing to the hostility of the powerful local family of the Tsrnojevich, and he returned to Hungary.

After the fall of the despotate the Turks besieged Belgrade which was defended by the Croat leader Ivan Talovats, and advanced into Hungary without success, the main fighting between them and the Hungarians under the leadership of Ivan Hunyadi taking place in Serbia. Hunyadi's success encouraged the Council of Buda to accept the proposal of the Papal legate and Brankovich for a mass attack against the Turks. An army under the leadership of Brankovich advanced as far as Sofia, but the onset of winter and hunger forced a halt to the advance and they were defeated by the Turks.

Murad was not in a position to take advantage of his victory because of the need to crush resistance among the Greeks and Albanians and was ready to agree to a 10 years truce, to come into existence only after having been agreed by the King and the Council in Hungary. Brankovich made a separate peace with the Sultan and was able to renew his rule over the despotate, one condition of peace being the return of the sons of captured Serbians. But the country was in ruins and Turkish officials retained control. Brankovich made an attempt to restore the old frontiers of the despotate, making peace with Stephen Vukchich who handed over the territory of Upper Zeta, and then began a war with Venice for the purpose of renewing his rule over the littoral of Zeta.

When in 1448 Ivan Hunyadi began preparations for a war with the Turks, Brankovich refused to take part on the grounds that the preparations had not been sufficiently planned. The Hungarian army marched through Serbia, plundering on the way and was completely defeated by the Turks at Kosovo. Fleeing to Smederov, Hunyadi was captured by the Serbians and the Hungarians had to pay 100,000 ducats – partly in compensation for the damage they had caused – and to promise not to enter Serbian territory unless such a move was necessary for the defence of the despotate.

The accession of Muhamed II was the signal for a new attack in the Balkans beginning with the capture of Constantinople in 1453 in which 1,500 troops of Brankovich fought with the Sultan's army. Brankovich hoped that by supporting the Sultan and at the same time reconciling himself with Hungary and Bosnia he could preserve the despotate. Muhamed, however, broke the peace between him and Brankovich and advanced on Serbia. Merchants of Dubrovnik, fleeing before the Turkish advance, described the devastation following in the wake of the victorious Turks; some 50,000 inhabitants were estimated to have been slain or enslaved. The greater part of the despotate, particularly the central area, was at the mercy of the Turks. In the following year the Turks advanced to Novo Brdo which was stormed – a promise to spare the inhabitants was not fulfilled. The result was the Turkish occupation of the whole southern area of the despotate. Deprived of the possibility of help from Hungary or Austria, Brankovich was forced to make peace. Muhamed continued his advance to Smederov but suffered a decisive defeat; the Turkish fleet on the Danube was destroyed by the ships of Ivan Hunyadi, while Serbian troops thwarted a Turkish attempt to capture Belgrade. The death of Hunyadi and the inability of Brankovich to continue the war on his own compelled him to make peace which was followed soon after by his death.

The death of Brankovich was followed by a struggle for the succession among the members of his own family and the Serbian nobles who were prepared to call in Hungarians and Turks in their support. The leader of the Turkophil group was Michael Andejelovich whose brother was a Turkish vassal. Michael persuaded Brankovich's son Lazar to make peace with the Turks in 1457 in return for which he obtained the whole of the despotate apart from Novo Brdo. Fearing that the Hungarians might seize Smederov, Michael let the Turks into the city. The anti-Turkish party hoped to drive out the Turks, imprison Michael, and proclaim their own candidate Stephen whose right had been confirmed by Mathias Korvin, King of Hungary. This was followed by the appearance of a Turkish army and Serbia again became a battlefield where Turks and Hungarians fought for supremacy. Muhamed Andelov, commanding a Turkish force, succeeded in seizing the whole of Serbia. The Hungarians arranged a marriage between the heir to the Bosnian throne and the daughter of Lazar, thus uniting Bosnia and Serbia. The marriage, solemnised in 1459, did not save Serbia which was proclaimed a sanjak.

CHAPTER V

The Serbians in Voivodina

THE DEFEAT OF BAJAZID AT ANGORA had increased the hopes of the Christians of the possibility of a final victory over the Turks. Immediately after the battle, Stephen Lazarevich, a reluctant participant in the battle from which he had managed to escape, went to Constantinople where the Emperor granted him the title of Despot, after which he returned home hoping for support from the West and especially Hungary which was most directly threatened by the Turks. Stephen's aims fitted in with the plans of Sigismund who was involved in internal problems and the forces of Stephen could be useful in securing the frontiers of Hungary against a Turkish attack. As a result of negotiations with Sigismund, Stephen was granted large properties in Hungary and as a further means of strengthening his powers Sigismund granted him the Bans of Belgrade and Machva, with the towns of Valjev, Sokol, Golubats, Smederov and part of the Banat. The Turkish advance led to the migration of members of the Serbian dynasty to Hungary, where they were given grants of lands. These included Dimitir, the son of King Vukashin, who was granted the town of Villagosh and established as Zupan of Zarandask.

Relations between Stephen and Sigismund remained close. When in 1411 Stephen renewed his oath to Sigismund he received more towns. These grants of territory made him one of the most powerful men in Hungary. Like the King he had his own treasury; in the Zupas he controlled he had the power to appoint and dismiss Zupans and sub-Zupans. Nevertheless he was vassal of the Hungarian king, obliged to maintain an army equal to that of the King, and to appear at court in the King's retinue. He took part in the coronation of Sigismund as King and in the Church Council in Kossnits in 1414.

In view of the advancing age of Stephen it became necessary to confirm the relationship with Hungary and settle the question of succession. This was arranged between the Despot and the King at Tati in 1426, negotiations vitally important for both parties, conscious as they were of the constant Turkish threat. The situation for Serbia was much more critical than for Hungary, more immediately threatened by the Turks and in no position to resist on its own. The Despot was faced with the need to accept Hungarian vassalage and was forced to agree to the return of Belgrade to the King, transferring the formal rights of the Hungarians into actual control of Serbia. George Brankovich was recognised as successor to Stephen, with little choice but to agree to the conditions laid down at Tati. So long as Belgrade remained in Christian hands the people of Serbia might hope for eventual liberation from Turkish rule, a hope which would strengthen their resolve to resist. The difficult situation which had forced the Serbians to accept domination had been worsened by the death of Stephen in 1427. Under the terms of the agreement of Tati, Belgrade and Machva and Golubats belonged to Hungary. As soon as he had received news of the death of Stephen, Sigismund hastened to Belgrade while George arrived from Zeta and the terms of the negotiations agreed at Tati were confirmed. Having obtained an oath of loyalty from George, Sigismund established him as 'princeps' and Despot of all Ras and Albania. In addition George inherited all the Hungarian possessions of his predecessor; indeed he succeeded in extending his territories and strengthened his friendship with the King by giving his daughter in marriage to Ulrich Celli, one of the most powerful magnates in Hungary. On the death of Sigismund he received further territories from his successor Albrecht.

George, following the example of Stephen, employed Serbians to govern his territories in Hungary, and this, along with the great power he enjoyed led to hostility among the Hungarian magnates and the hierarchy of the Catholic Church. As an Orthodox Christian, George nevertheless exercised his rights as ruler over the Catholic churches in the territories under his control. Those Hungarians who disapproved of his powers and his custom of appointing Serbians to positions of importance tried to prevent his acquisition of further territories and in 1439 the Despot and his son-in-law were forbidden to employ foreigners. In the same year George suffered another setback when the Turks for the first time seized Serbia and deprived him of his territories outside Hungary. His relations with the new Hungarian King Ladislav were unfriendly. In 1440 Ladislav seized from the Despot, allegedly on the grounds of treason, the towns of Debretsin and Besermey. Relations were to some extent improved when George recognised Ladislav as his superior. Relations with Janko Hunyadi, one of the most powerful men in Hungary – thought by his contemporaries to be the natural son of Sigismund – were equally unfriendly. In order to persuade Hunyadi to reach agreement with the Turks the Despot ceded to him the town of Vilogosh. Despite this concession relations between the two men deteriorated; Hunyadi was anxious for war with the Turks, George was equally anxious to maintain the peace and he did not take part in the war which followed in which the Hungarians were defeated at the Battle of Varna where Ladislav was killed. It was easy for Hunyadi to attribute the defeat to the treachery of George, which provided him with a pretext to deprive the Despot of some of his territories. The Despot was more conscious of Turkish strength than was Hunyadi and was determined not to become involved in a war which if successful could only benefit Hungary. Consequently when in 1448 Hunyadi was preparing for war, not only did George fail to support him but he informed the Sultan of the Hungarian preparations and Hunyadi was decisively defeated at Kosovo. Hunyadi was captured by George and held until he promised to pay 100,000 ducats in compensation for the damage he had caused and restored the lands which he had seized from the Despot in Hungary. Hunyadi was forced to accept these terms but he did not forget; having purchased his freedom he took his revenge on the Despot, particularly at the expense of George's territories in Hungary, to which the Despot replied with 'dire threats'. In fact these threats were empty; not only was he forced to retreat but to pay 155,000 ducats and hand over some of his territories to the sons of Hunyadi.

The knowledge that the Turks were preparing an attack on Belgrade led the Christians momentarily to sink their differences and prepare for joint action. A meeting was called at which George was present along with Hunyadi and the Franciscan Friar John Capistrini and representatives from the West. Capistrini was mainly concerned with the problem of 'schismatism' and forcing the Despot to renounce his 'heresy' and join the Catholic Church. This can be confirmed from a letter which Capistrini sent to the Pope, according to which George claimed to have received from the previous Pope Nicholas V permission to build Greek monasteries in Hungary. According to Capistrini, George was persecuting Catholics and forcing them to embrace Orthodoxy, imprisoning those who refused. Capistrini further maintained that George had rejected the request of the Friar on the grounds that though he was a vassal of the 'apostolic' King of Hungary, he was not prepared to buy support at the price of renouncing the faith of his ancestors and he refused to attend the Councils of Basle and Ferrara at which even the Byzantine Emperor was present.

While the council was in progress the Sultan's army invaded Serbia and seized Novo Brdo, and George was forced to accept a humiliating peace which he was not fated to enjoy for long. Faced with the constant threat from the Turks he now found himself under attack from Hunyadi whose armies attacked Belgrade and captured the Despot, keeping him imprisoned until he had paid the sum of 60,000 ducats. With his death and the capture of Smederov by the Turks the despotate of Serbia came to an end. The despots as rulers of Serbia ceased to exist although the title continued to be used until Hungary itself fell to the Turks. The first to hold the title after the death of George was Vuk whose origins were obscure. He first appears in history as a member of an embassy from the Sultan bringing an offer of peace to the King of Hungary. This offer was rejected by Mathias but the King invited Vuk to enter the royal service in order to defend Hungary against the Turks and 'other enemies', including the Poles. As a reward for his successful efforts against the Turks he was granted territories and the title of Despot in 1471 and some of the lands held by the Despot George. Vuk played a distinguished part in the Turko-Hungarian wars in the years 1475 and 1476. When Mathias seized Shabats, Vuk advanced to Srebnits in Bosnia, attacking the towns and killing some 500 Turks, and succeeded in capturing the important town of Svornik. One result was the mass Serbian emigration to Srem. At the beginning of August it was learned that the Turks under the leadership of the Beg of Smederov had crossed the Danube and were pillaging the area around Temishvar. An army was despatched under the leadership of Vuk to Banat which succeeded in halting the Turkish advance and capturing some 300 Turks who were handed over to the King. Encouraged by this victory an attempt was made by Vuk to recapture Smederov without success. He forced the Turks to evacuate the town and withdraw to the fortresses, and his army settled down to a long siege but the arrival of Turkish reinforcements forced him to abandon the project.

It was inevitable that the Serbians should be drawn into the struggle for the succession in Hungary and Vuk took part in the wars between Mathias and the Emperor Frederick, a war in which the Serbians acquired an unenviable reputation for their plundering in Austria. In 1480 he was in action against the Turks advancing towards Sarajevo. His task was to maintain and secure the route for the passage of a Christian army across the Danube. The Christian victory over the Turkish fleet was followed by the capture of the towns of Branichev and Krushevats, and large numbers of the inhabitants emigrated to Banat and settled in the areas around Temishvar. In 1483 Vuk acted as negotiator in the peace talks between Mathias and the Sultan; we do not know why the Sultan entrusted the mission to him. Vuk was anxious to obtain from the Sultan the former Serbian lands, and may have hoped to achieve this by his success in negotiating a peace favourable to the Turks. In a letter to the Sultan, Vuk begged Bajazid to discontinue the building of forts in 'his' territories and halt his advance towards Hungary because the King Mathias wanted peace on the basis of brotherhood and friendship (bratsvo i prijateljstvo). The letter concluded with the words 'may God grant your imperial majesty long life and may we serve you rightly and truly – and may God strengthen your empire'. In another letter he describes himself as the slave (rob) of the Emperor. His attempts to conclude peace between the King and the Sultan proved unsuccessful and a Turkish army from Bosnia advanced through Croatia to Kranjsk and Korushak, pillaging and enslaving its inhabitants. The Turks were intercepted on their return by an army led by Vuk and the Ban of Croatia and decisively defeated. In 1485 Vuk died without heirs. Some years before his death, Stephen, the blind son of the Despot, had also died. After the fall of the Serbian state Stephen had gone abroad to await better days. In 1461 he had married Angelina, the sister-in-law of the Albanian Skenderberg, and settled in the territories of the Republic of Venice with his three sons, George, Mario and John. On the death of Vuk, Mathias invited Angelina and her sons to Buda and the eldest was proclaimed Despot and granted the lands of Srem, Slankamen and Kupnik. George enjoyed the sympathy of the court; through the influence of Mathias he married Isabella of Aragon of the dynasty of Naples, the nearest relative of the Hungarian queen. According to one source he tried to persuade his wife to give up her Catholic 'heresy', which may have been one of the reasons why the couple separated. Another reason may have been the hostility which developed between George and the widow of the King after the death of Mathias. In the struggle for the succession George and his brother began by supporting Ivanish, the illegitimate son of Mathias, then switched their allegiance to the Emperor Frederick, finally backing Ladislav Jagellon. In 1493, probably as a reward for the services he had rendered Ladislav, John was granted the title of Despot.

Although their mother was Catholic and their childhood had been passed among Catholics, the brothers were from 'the seed of Nemanje' and they, along with their mother, strongly supported the idea of a Serbian state and the Orthodox Church. Meanwhile the position of the Serbians in Hungary was steadily deteriorating. The weak King Ladislav deprived the Serbians of lands granted by Mathias which had been freed from the payment of tithes to the Catholic Church. This privilege was now withdrawn. George had already quarrelled with the Catholic Archbishop over the question in 1496. His plea that the Serbians should be freed from this obligation was answered by the Archbishop; the money was required for the defence of Hungary and it was the duty of the Despot to contribute to this defence and support the Catholic Church for 'God created the Christian lands of Hungary and not schismatics' and the Despot did not have the right to maintain a separate Serbian state in it. 'In a Christian state one must live according to the Christian laws.' It was probably after this that George entered a monastery. He was succeeded by his brother John who was more suited to the position. In the wars against the Turks John was the main commander on the southern frontier, carrying out military operations around Smederov then in Bosnia around Svornik, apparently with some success since he returned with booty and prisoners. He was also involved in the wars between the Turks and Venice; in view of the advantages this offered him he sent his brother Mario to Venice to persuade the Senate to continue the fight; the mission failed, however, since peace was concluded with the Turks. The Turks had captured Lepanto and the Venetians sent an ambassador to Constantinople to sue for peace. The terms demanded by Bajazid were unacceptable to the Venetians and were rejected, and the armies of the Sultan captured Modone. In spite of the Turkish capture of Cepholonia and Ithaca, however, no further gains were made by either side, and peace was concluded in 1503, leaving the Turks in control of the entire coast of the Peleponnese. In the same year John died leaving two daughters, but no son or male heir except his brother Mario who refused to accept the title of Despot offered by Ladislav, whereupon the King took over the territories of the Brankovich family. In 1513 Mario became Metropolitan of Belgrade, controlling the Serbians in Srem and those living in the vicinity of Belgrade and perhaps Hungary as well.

The title of Despot was finally granted to the Croat Ivanish Berislavich; his task was to aid the King in the defence of the southern frontier particularly Srem. In 1509 he entered into negotiations with the Ban of Belgrade, George Kanizaje, for joint action against the Turks but nothing came of it, possibly because the Turks were aware of the plan, and fighting broke out for some reason between Berislavich and Kanizaje. A proposed attack against Dalmatia likewise came to nothing. At the beginning of 1514 Berislavich died; he had married the widow of John by whom he had two sons, the eldest of whom, Stephen, was named as Despot (1514-35).

In 1514 the Hungarian Archbishop announced, with the consent of the Pope, a Holy War against the Turks. The urban poor, artisans and impecunious nobles joined forces with the peasants, responding enthusiastically to the call in the hope of turning the situation to their advantage. Owing to the fact that the organisation of the army was weak, lacking money and food, the troops turned to plunder, while the obvious weakness of the leadership encouraged the peasants to hope for an improvement in their position. The Hungarian nobles, distrustful of the idea of a Crusade from the beginning, and fearful of the armed might of the peasants, persuaded the Archbishop to call a halt to further recruitment. Serbians were involved in those areas where they were mixed with the Hungarians. The attitude of the Serbian leaders was divided, some supporting the barons others the peasants. The leader of the peasants was George Dozsa, originally entrusted with the command of the army, now identifying himself with the peasants and declaring war against the 'oppressers of the people'. In the reprisals which followed the defeat of the rebels the Serbians suffered severely.

The years which followed were difficult for the Despot Stephen Berislavich. The Sultan was preparing an attack against Hungary; reaching the Danube and the Sava he began the construction of a bridge across the latter river; though the rising of the river damaged the bridge it only delayed the Turkish advance for about a week. The Turks advanced into Srem, destroying the main towns before withdrawing, while on his return Stephen attempted to restore the ruined fortresses. In 1522 he sent an embassy to the Palatin Istvan Bathory informing him of the State of the frontier. His request for money to pay his mercenaries met with a cool response from the King since the royal treasury was empty. In the spring of 1526 word was received that the Sultan was advancing towards Hungary through Belgrade. The Battle of Mohacs in the same year, in which the Hungarians were defeated, was one of the greatest disasters in Hungarian history. The King Ladislav II was killed on the battlefield, Stephen had been entrusted with the defence of Slavonia and escaped the fate of the King. After the battle he rejected an offer from John Nenad (see below) for joint action against the Turks, either because of the dubious origins of Nenad or from envy. In a separate action he defeated the Turks, largely because Suleiman was involved in fighting in the Near East at that period, and seized a number of towns.

The death of Ladislav was followed in Hungary by a struggle for the succession. The claim of Ferdinand of Habsburg was backed by his sister, the widow of Ladislav, and an attempt was made to enlist the aid of Stephen. Stephen demanded money for the maintenance of a force of 1,000 cavalry and a fortified town where his mother and two sisters could be assured of safety in the event of towns being captured by the Turks. For his brother he demanded the title of 'prepositor' and the towns of Mitrovits and Vrdnik which he hoped to seize. If the Catholic Archbishop should demand the latter town for himself, Stephen should be paid for the expense involved in its capture. Provided these conditions were fulfilled he was ready at his own expense to maintain a naval force on the Sava. The difficult situation in which Ferdinand found himself forced him to accept these conditions. In 1527 Stephen was present at the Council in Buda which Ferdinand had chosen for his capital.

The main rival of Ferdinand was Isvan Zapolyai who, as soon as the Turkish army had withdrawn from the country, was crowned King by his adherents. Ferdinand, supported with money obtained from the Fuggers, organised an army and expelled Zapolyai. The decision of the latter to seek the support of the Sultan was serious for Stephen, whose territories were directly exposed to Turkish attack. The support of the Sultan was conditional on Zapolyai accepting the position of vassal. It is true that Ferdinand granted Stephen the right to hold and defend the towns which had been held by John Nenad, but this was insufficient for the defence of the frontiers. More urgent was the need for money to pay his troops; the appeals to Ferdinand proved fruitless largely because the King had no money to spare. The gravity of the situation was fully realised at court, but in view of the imminent threat to Vienna, all available money was required for the defence of the capital, and an embassy sent to obtain money could only provide enough for 200 mercenaries and a promise of 4,000 forints which, however, failed to materialise. A plea to Bathory proved equally unsuccessful, despite the warnings from Stephen that the Turks 'would plunder the land and the whole kingdom would be lost'. Before such a powerful force he felt himself 'like a drop on the ocean'. He proposed to make a personal visit to Vienna but was dissuaded by his advisers. The sum of 300 forints which he ultimately received was totally inadequate for his needs; at the beginning of 1529, therefore, he evacuated the towns of Bach and Feledzhaz which were immediately occupied by the Turks. Thus Bach, the most important fortress in southern Hungary, fell to the Turks without a struggle and the way was open to Buda. To Ferdinand, who had rejected all pleas for help, this seemed an act of treason, and the Despot and his mother were arrested. This task was entrusted to John Hoberdanets, whose instructions were to win over those Serbian leaders who supported Zapolyai, a task he seems to have carried out successfully. Stephen did not regard himself as guilty, made no effort to escape, and remained faithful to Ferdinand. The royal Council took the view that he should be set at liberty, but this view was opposed by the King at a time when the Turks were advancing towards Buda. This was a view shared by Hoberdanets who feared Stephen's revenge at some future date. How important this fear was can be seen from the fact that Ferdinand promised that if Stephen were released no harm would come to Hoberdanets. Stephen fled to the Turkish camp and offered his services to the Sultan who granted him the rule of his former territories in Srem and Slavonia. The Despot then entered into friendly relations with Zapolyai; when some members of the family of Hoberdanets fell into the hands of Zapolyai, the Despot, presumably with the approval of the latter, gave orders for their death. Hoberdanets not unnaturally blamed Zapolyai for this deed and attempted without success to have him killed. The death by drowning in the Danube, whether by accident or design, removed him from the scene.

In 1530 Stephen carried out an attack against the followers of Ferdinand, but by 1531 he was attempting to re-establish friendly relations with the King. By 1532 the situation had changed. The Emperor Charles V attempted to win over Stephen and the supporters of Zapolyai to join his brother, promising them an amnesty in the name of Ferdinand. This action was too late because the Sultan's army was advancing towards Hungary and

Stephen was waiting with a force of some 200 cavalry to join it. In a fight between him and the Beg of Smederov, the reasons for which are unknown, Stephen was killed in 1536.

Among the Serbian leaders in Hungary Radich Bozich was the one who would probably have succeeded Stephen. On the death of Ladislav II, Radich had joined forces with Zapolyai and was granted the title of Despot on the occasion of Zapolyai's coronation. The title itself was largely meaningless since it did not carry with it any lands. In 1527, however, Radich died. Thus it was Paul Bakich who succeeded Stephen as Despot. Like other Serbian leaders Bakich had submitted to the Sultan in an effort to preserve his territories. He was ready to go to Hungary provided he were granted lands equal in value to those he had held in Serbia. In 1526, knowing of the Sultan's preparations for an attack on Hungary he moved there with his family. Once the question of territories had been settled Bakich advanced with his army to Srem to undertake the defence of the border against the Turks. He took part in the Battle of Mohacs in which his brother was killed. In the struggle for the succession which followed the death of Ladislav, Bakich gave his support to Zapolyai, and was present at his coronation, but changed sides after the defeat of the latter and remained faithful to Ferdinand to the end of his life.

In co-operation with Valentin Terek he began operations against Zapolyai in northern Hungary for which he was rewarded with territories for his services to the Christian faith. In 1528 he was put in command of the Danube fleet. This was no easy job; there was no money in the treasury and the situation was worse for the Serbians than for the Hungarian fleet, and Bakich asked to be relieved of his post. In May he went personally to Buda to acquaint the Council with the situation. But his request for money was rejected on the grounds that none was available. Bakich then informed the King of the Council's refusal to supply him with money and Ferdinand instructed the latter to make at least some payment but without success. Bakich claimed that many Serbians were eager to leave Serbia and settle in Hungary to take up the struggle against the Turks but only if they could be assured of their future, and were looking to him, Bakich, for advice. There was growing dissatisfaction among the men in the fleet. Roughly half of the ships making up the Danube fleet were Serbian and these later negotiated with the leaders of the Turkish fleet and joined with them in an attack against the Hungarians, most of whom were killed. In the same year the Turks took Buda. Bakich took part in resisting the Turkish advance to Vienna but in view of the superior naval strength of the Turkish fleet he was unable to prevent them constructing a bridge over the river.

In 1530 the Serbians from Srem inquired through Bakich whether they could rely on Ferdinand to defend them; if so he should send them at least

200 cavalry and an equivalent number of infantry, in which case they were prepared to attack the Turks. Bakich assured the King that large numbers of Serbians were ready to enter his services, and if their complaints were met, those sailors who had deserted to the enemy would be ready to return to his support. Ferdinand made some vague promises but nothing more. He was awaiting the outcome of the negotiations between the Turks and Zapolyai. Nevertheless since the emigration of the Serbians was a matter of vital importance to him, he arranged a secret meeting with Bakich, the gist of which was a promise that the Serbians would be freed from Turkish enslavement. Bakich was asked to resume command of the fleet but he excused himself on the grounds that he had more urgent matters to deal with elsewhere, without specifying what these were.

When the Christian army assembled at Vienna, Bakich received from the Pope a consecrated banner, and played a distinguished and successful part in the defence of the city. In 1532 he represented Ferdinand in negotiations with Zapolyai. In 1532 he received the town of Sombathelj, in 1533 the customs of Ujvar, and in the following year he was confirmed in the possession of the territories he held for his lifetime with right of succession. As his power and influence grew he made many enemies, not the least of them being the Queen Maria. He warned Ferdinand that some of his closest associates were negotiating with Zapolyai, but this was not believed, though Bakich was in fact correct.

Acting on the advice of Bakich, Ferdinand prepared an attack against the Turks, the plan being to deal with them first before attacking Zapolyai whose main support came from the Sultan. The Serbians in Srem on hearing of the plan assured Bakich that the entire population would rise in his support. Ferdinand ordered the Serbians to submit to General Katsijaner, while Bakich with his army should remain in western Hungary to defend the frontier against Zapolyai. Bakich's main aim was to take part in the fighting against the Turks and Ferdinand gave him command of some 2,000 cavalry consisting mainly of Serbians. In order to strengthen his authority over the Serbians Ferdinand granted Bakich the title of Despot. This was a matter of very little significance. Whether Bakich ever recognised the title and whether the Serbians in Turkish territory were aware of it is not known. In 1536 Bakich was killed by the Turks at Goriana. With his death the title of Despot disappeared and with it even the shadow of a Serbian state for 300 years.

'Tsar' John Nenad

The rise of this somewhat mysterious figure was due in part to the fact that both claimants to the throne of Hungary were eager to win his support. His origins were obscure; according to the English ambassador, whom he seems to have impressed, no-one knew of his past, 'who his family were, where he was born, but simply that he had been sent by God'. According to one source he was a direct descendent of the Despot; another source attributed his descent from the Byzantine emperors. His contemporaries accepted the version that if he was not descended from the Despot he was at least a Serbian. Nenad modestly claimed to be a prophet sent by God with the mission to carry out 'great things' including the extirpation of heresy and paganism. The first accurate information we have of him is after the Battle of Mohacs. Having attracted the support of the poor he had a powerful army which both Ferdinand and Zapolyai were anxious to enlist in the struggle for the succession. The first offer was made by Zapolyai who invited him to Tokay when Nenad expressed his willingness to carry out the wishes of the King. In 1526 he advanced to Srem and seized some towns from the Turks. Wishing to continue fighting but lacking cannon he turned to Stephen Berislavich for help, a request rejected by the Despot who was unwilling to act in conjunction with Nenad, seeing him perhaps as a potential rival as leader of the Serbians. Nenad then proceeded to expel the Turks from Subotnits which had belonged to the Hungarian Valentin Terek, and was now occupied by the forces of Nenad which defeated Terek when he attempted to recover his lands. These victories of Nenad alarmed the Hungarian nobles since it was clear that he was not liberating these territories with the object of restoring them to their former owners. When in the course of the campaign Nenad captured the territories formerly in the possession of Ladislav Chakiije, the latter was completely defeated when he attempted to recover them. Relations between Nenad and the Hungarian nobles steadily deteriorated. When the danger from the Turks seemed less acute the nobles made an attempt to regain their lands. Nenad maintained that he had found the lands deserted, that he had captured them with his own people (sa svojom narodom) and implied that he meant to keep them. The nobles defended themselves on the grounds that they had been forced to leave them because of the Turks. Failing to reach agreement with Nenad, the nobles complained to Zapolyai alleging that he was doing nothing to defend their interests. Zapolyai, however, lacked the power to intervene. He summoned Nenad to meet him but the latter refused a personal meeting, sending a delegate who defended Nenad's actions and convinced Zapolyai of Nenad's loyalty. When Terek again advanced against Nenad, Zapolyai could only warn him of the danger he faced.

Nenad's power continued to increase to the point where he controlled a force of some 10,000 men, more than either Ferdinand or Zapolyai could match. As his power increased so did his pretentions; his followers addressed him as Tsar, somewhat less modestly he styled himself as Emperor of Constantinople, and like other rulers he made grants of lands to his followers. Lacking the means to maintain such a large army he resorted to requisition and downright robbery without distinguishing between Hungarian and Turk. The more powerful he became – and it is an indication of his power that ambassadors from France and England attended him – the more essential it was for both sides in the succession struggle to win his support. But while Zapolyai was anxious to maintain the support of Nenad – if only to prevent him turning to Ferdinand – the nobles supporting Zapolyai and the Catholic Church along with the voivod Peter Perenje remained distrustful of him. On the other hand Ferdinand, lacking any real power base in Hungary, was anxious to win Nenad to his side. His sister Maria acted as intermediary and entrusted Hoberdanets with gifts to Nenad in an effort to persuade him to switch allegiance. Nenad's acceptance was conditional on his receiving arms and money from Ferdinand. Under pressure from Maria these conditions were accepted by Ferdinand who, in a letter to Nenad, expressed his satisfaction with his offer of loyalty. Nenad did not obtain the title of Despot which was already held by Stephen Berislavich, but it is an indication of the importance which Ferdinand attributed to him that the King addressed him as 'illustrious' a form of address confined only to members of the ruling house.

Nenad's power now began to deteriorate. He underestimated the strength of Zapolyai and Ferdinand was too far away to render effective aid, his own forces were now too weak and this combined with his lack of money made further large scale action impossible. Zapolyai, however, was still hoping to persuade Nenad to change sides. Nenad retorted that Zapolyai had failed to provide any assistance whereas Ferdinand had done so much for him that he could not abandon the King. Zapolyai sent Radich Bozich to Nenad in an effort to persuade him to change his mind but without success. He had to face the fact that he was now threatened by a union of the armies of Ferdinand and Nenad. On the other hand Zapolyai had the support of the Hungarian nobles and the Catholic Church, and the offensive against Nenad took the form of a Holy War. Peter Perenje with an army of some 12,000 men prepared to attack Nenad. Nenad appealed to Perenje: 'why do you gather such an army against us Serbians? Are we not also Christians? Would it not be better to unite against the pagans (Turks)?' Perenje rejected the offer of friendship made by Nenad; it was a fatal mistake. His army was almost completely annihilated; the Hungarian losses were greater than those suffered at Mohacs. The significance of this victory lay in the fact that it was a Serbian victory over the Hungarians, perhaps the only occasion where the Serbians could claim to be defending their interests rather than the interests of Hungary and its rulers, 'a Serbian victory' as it was described in the chronicles.

Perenje's defeat was a serious blow to Zapolyai, particularly after his failure to reach agreement with Ferdinand, and he made one more attempt to win Nenad to his side. Nenad was in the favourable position of having both sides bidding for his support. He demanded troops and money from Ferdinand, but the King was now doubtful whether Nenad could long survive to continue the fight against Zapolyai, and demanded his submission. Hoberdanets, who was entrusted with the mission to Nenad, appears to have been successful in obtaining the allegiance of Nenad's troops, and instructed them that if any misfortune should befall Nenad they should assemble between the Danube and the Theiss and await the arrival of Ferdinand. The relations between Zapolyai and Nenad were now openly hostile and the latter forbade his followers to pay taxes to Zapolyai and issued a proclamation to the followers of the latter: 'Tsar John the servant of God sends to all Hungarians faithful to Christ his greetings. It has come to our knowledge that John (Zapolyai) has not hesitated to deprive them (the Hungarians) of their liberty which the mercy of Christ has granted to his flock, and is taxing them to pay money to the Sultan to help him to gain the crown of Hungary'. Nenad then begged them not to 'shed their blood for unbelievers' for 'the hour of delivery is at hand'. Ferdinand 'the undefeated and legitimate ruler of Hungary' would soon liberate this 'unhappy land'.

Ferdinand naturally welcomed this open declaration of support and he called on Nenad to prevent the Turks coming to the aid of Zapolyai. Zapolyai did not remain inactive; his main strength lay in Erdelj where it was not difficult to arouse hostility to Nenad. Under the leadership of Perenje an army consisting largely of troops from Upper Hungary and Erdelj was raised for action against Nenad. In the ensuing battle Nenad's army suffered a crushing defeat, losing some 8,000 men, mostly infantry. At this time two ambassadors from Nenad, John Dolich and Fabian were with Ferdinand in Vienna. Hoberdanets advised the King to release Dolich but to detain Fabian, probably with the object of maintaining pressure on Nenad to continue the fight, for the consequences of this defeat were serious for Ferdinand. The changes in the fortune of Zapolyai which followed the victory over Nenad led some of Ferdinand's supporters to desert him; these included Valentin Terek. Ferdinand at first refused to believe the news of Nenad's defeat. He was less concerned with the personal fate of Nenad than with the need to keep his army in being, and when he at last realised the full extent of the catastrophe his first aim was to salvage what could be saved from the wreckage. Since Nenad was unable to prevent the union of the army of Erdelj with Zapolyai, Ferdinand instructed him to meet with his army at Buda and subdue the area between the Danube and the Theiss in order to defend the frontier against the Turks.

While the main object of Nenad was to rebuild his strength, the object of his enemies was to attack him before this could be achieved. Zapolyai, however, had not abandoned hope of winning Nenad to his side, and to this end he employed the services of the French ambassador who was attempting to create an anti-Habsburg coalition. Ferdinand countered by instructing Hoberdanets to have the ambassador arrested promising rich rewards if he were successful. Similar rewards were promised to Nenad with an assurance that the King was ready with an army to advance towards Hungary, at the same time despatching ships to the Danube. He expressed the hope that Nenad would be 'courageous' because he was 'long convinced that yours are the most loyal and courageous warriors'. He also warned him against engaging in battle with Perenje unless he were sure of success. Nenad accepted the King's advice; leaving a force to guard his territories on the Danube and Theiss he advanced with his army to Buda. On the way he stopped at Segedon where according to reports the population, young and old, barricaded themselves in their homes. One citizen seems to have been bolder, however, for as Nenad was walking in the street he was shot and fatally wounded in 1527.

Rightly or wrongly Nenad has become a Serbian national hero. After the disappearance of the despotate of Serbia, those who bore the title of Despot were pawns in the struggle between Hungarians and Turks, their task being to defend the frontiers against Turkish attacks. This was a struggle which the Serbians could not win. In fact the Turkish victories over the Hungarians ensured 300 years of Turkish domination over the Serbians, in which only the Church helped to maintain a sense of national identity. A complete Hungarian victory, permanently removing the Turkish threat, would have been almost as disastrous for the Serbians. The Hungarian kings had always been the main enemies of Serbia; so long as Hungary was menaced by the Turks the rulers of Hungary might be prepared to permit the Serbians in Hungary a wide latitude, e.g. the maintenance of the Orthodox Church. It is unlikely that religious liberty would have survived the removal of the Turkish threat. The Serbians as a nation could hardly have survived the disappearance of their Church which preserved the language and traditions of the people till the day of liberation. In losing their freedom the Serbians saved Europe from the Turks and preserved Christian civilisation. Europe remained unimpressed.

CHAPTER VI

Church, State and Economy

As IN ALL MEDIEVAL STATES the Church occupied an important and privileged position in the Serbian lands; nobles could be deprived of their lands at any time, while Church lands were inalienable although transferable within the Church. On the other hand neither monks nor clergy could leave the Church. The Church was a useful counter-balance between the ruler and the over-mighty subject. One feature of the Church in Serbia which differentiated it from those of neighbouring states lay in the close links it maintained with the ruling family. Sava, the son of Stephen Nemanje, Stephen himself and his son Stephen First Crowned, all ended as monks, Sava becoming first Archbishop of Serbia. The Archbishop's title was similar to that of the King, 'by the grace of God, Archbishop of all the Serbian lands'. The Church had separated from the autocephalous Church of Ohrid, and, following the capture of Constantinople in 1206 and the virtual collapse of the Greek Empire, permission had been granted from the Patriarch of Nicea for the establishment of an independent archbishopric in Serbia. The Archbishop was chosen by the King, generally by a Council in the presence of the nobles and clergy, not always in accordance with canon law which stated that only a bishop could be appointed as archbishop, thus legally debarring Sava from the position since he was only a monk. The first capital of the Archbishop was at the monastery of Zich, which in the course of the 13th century was destroyed probably as a result of fighting, and the seat was transferred to Pech. Archbishops, however, frequently travelled abroad. On serious occasions the King would take an oath in the presence of the Archbishop as happened on the conclusion of peace with Dubrovnik, in 1254, and the negotiations between Dushan and Cantacuzene in 1342.

From its foundation the Church in Serbia had recognised the authority of the Patriarch of Constantinople who while in exile had granted Serbia its archbishopric. When Dushan became Emperor he raised the archbishopric to the rank of Patriarchate of Serbia and the Greeks, which led to break with Constantinople and a schism which lasted till 1375. At the same time seven new archbishoprics were founded, greatly extending the influence of the Church throughout the land; these included Zeta, Ras (the only one under the jurisdiction of Ohrid), Hvost, Hum and Toplits. Since these were all small towns the seat of the archbishoprics lay in the monasteries.

Of the possessions of the bishops, which at that time were inferior to those of the monasteries, we know only from the charters of Urosh I to the Bishop of Hum, and Urosh III to the Bishop of Prizren. Urosh I granted to the church in Ston many villages in 'the land of Hum'. In another charter he made grants to the monastery of the Apostle Peter in Lim. Bishops were not slow to take advantage of the acts of generosity; Danilo, Bishop of Hum, assured Urosh II of the parlous state of the bishopric and asserted that the only remedy lay in the King granting him the Church of the Apostles Peter and Paul and some other churches with their possessions. To the Bishop of Prizren, Urosh granted the town of Prizren with the Church of St. Nicholas. It was the duty of the Bishop to see that the peasants preserved the towns. Dushan handed over the fortresses to the newly founded monastery of Prizren and three villages to the Bishop.

One special feature of the monastic order were the so-called 'king's monasteries' which were under the direct control of the bishops. The Code of Dushan makes frequent references to Church matters, and to the duty of the protopop or presbyter to defend Orthodoxy: 'and the great Church (i.e. the Patriarch of Constantinople) shall appoint protopops to bring back Christians from the Latin heresy'. The Exarch, in accordance with the Byzantine custom, was concerned with church buildings, questions of liturgy and dress. The Code laid down that the Exarch could only be a monk. In Serbia monasteries enjoyed high standing; in Bulgaria and Byzantium they were to be found grouped together, but in Serbia they were isolated with widely scattered properties in the manner of Hungary, Italy and Germany. The tipik of Studenica included six monasteries, among them St. George in Ras and St. Nicholas in Toplits, both royal foundations, a custom followed by all Serbian rulers of the Nemanje dynasty.

It was inevitable that the Church in Serbia should follow the organisation of the Byzantine Church – the adoption of the 'Emperor's monasteries' free from episcopal supervision and under the direct control of the Patriarch. In Serbia four king's monasteries were allocated directly to the archbishops; Studenica, whose igumen had superiority over all others, the monastery of St. George in Ras, Grats and Hilander. To these was joined the monastery of Zich, the seat of the Archbishop, to whom Stephen First Crowned granted lands in the surrounding areas in Hvost and Zeta at Lake Ohrid. On the foundation of the bishoprics the seats were transferred to monasteries; the Bishop of Hvost had his see in the monastery of Little Studenica, the see of the Bishop of Zeta lay in a monastery near the sea in the small island of Prevlits, the Bishop of Hum had his see in the monastery of Ston.

The number of royal foundations increased after 1300 beginning with the monastery of St. Stephen between Ras and Kosovo founded by Milutin and Dragutin. Stephen Urosh founded the monastery of Decan, from which he acquired the name Stephen Decanski. The steady expansion of the Serbian frontiers in the south brought a number of older monasteries effectively under Serbian control, particularly in Macedonia. Urosh III created a new building for the monastery of St. George in Sarajevo. The Bulgarian Tsar Constantin Asen (1258-77) confirmed and renewed the privileges of the monastery. In charters issued in 1299 and 1300 Urosh proclaimed all previous charters concerning the monastery, whether Bulgarian or Greek, to be now invalid. Three persons were chosen to produce a new charter which would go beyond that of Constantin Asen: Sava, igumen of Studenica, Nicola Oparesta (probably a Serbian courtier) and the King's *dijak* Dabish. The charter included the names of the founders of the monastery including those of Stephen First Crowned, Constantin Asen, Urosh I and Andronicus II.

The influence of the rulers as founders of the monasteries was considerable. The igumen of the 'royal monasteries' was chosen by the King. In the Church of Decan the King had his own seat on which only he could sit. The Patriarch and Emperor appointed the igumen of the Archangel in Prizren. By order of Dushan, monks born in the villages had to go to another area in order to prevent the growth of family influence. Apart from the rulers many of the nobles made gifts to the monasteries for the repose of their souls. There are few references to monasteries for women apart from Ras and Toplits. Nuns had to live in monasteries, not in their own homes; an exception was made in the case of the widows of rulers who were permitted if they so wished to remain at court as was the custom at Constantinople.

Among the foundations outwith Serbia, by far the most important was that of Hilander on Mount Athos, the spiritual centre of the Orthodox world, founded by Nemanje in 1198. From small beginnings under the first Nemanjes it grew rapidly under Dushan. Dushan's liberality to Athos was not the result of his piety but was based on the need to win support from the Greek clergy. 'Recognition would constitute not only recognition and support by all the Byzantine subjects of his new state but would also provide religious sanction for his rule.' After the conquest of Serres, Dushan sent a mission to Athos with the object of obtaining recognition from the monks. In a chrysobul dated November 1345 he asked the monks to pray for him, in return for which he granted their request that the name of the Emperor should be commemorated before that of the Serbian king, and that the Holy

Mountain should be administered in accordance with its own rules and customs. The properties belonging to Mount Athos should not be given to Serbians. All possessions should be exempt from taxes and other obligations, the last being of particular importance. This charter set out the general principles on which the relations between Dushan and Mount Athos should be based; it was followed by others dealing with individual monasteries. One example is the charter granted to the monastery of Iviron, in which Dushan suspended the payment of 400 perpers which the monastery had been obliged to pay for its possessions at Radolivo, exempted all monastic possessions from taxes and corvee, and forbade his officials to demand taxes. At first sight the concession granted to the monks of naming the Emperor first may seem rather curious. It has been suggested by Soloviev (Dushan and Mount Athos) that Dushan recognised a certain 'moral authority in the legitimate empire'. On the other hand it may be that Dushan, already planning to assume the imperial title and eventual rule over the Empire, was simply stressing the priority of the imperial over the kingly title. The demands of the monks are understandable. Dushan was defacto ruler of Athos; he would not necessarily remain so. It would be unwise to alienate Cantacuzene. As it happened they recognised the Serbian Patriarchate, anathemised by the Patriarch of Constantinople, and a delegate from Athos attended the coronation of Dushan as Emperor. In the following year Dushan with his wife and son visited Mount Athos, the prohibition against women being waived on this occasion; further gifts were made to Hilander. It is possible that a further reason for the liberality of Dushan towards Mount Athos was to win support among the Hesycasts, a mystical group associated with the name of Gregorius Palamas, Archbishop of Salonika, who were numerous at Athos and strongly supported Cantacuzene. As a result of Dushan's conquests the autocephalous Church of Ohrid was now in Serbian hands, and the Archbishop Nicola took part in the coronation of Dushan and in the council at Skopje in 1347.

In the Slav areas of the Adriatic the Catholic Church was dominant, especially as a result of the creation of the archbishopric of Bar, which had been founded without Papal approval though this was ultimately granted. In addition Dubrovnik obtained an Archbishop but here the position was not clear. The archbishopric had been obtained from King Michael but Dubrovnik later claimed control of all the territories of Bar, but failed to substantiate the claim and the final victory went to Bar. The eastern lands of the Great Zupan belonged to the Archbishop of Ohrid, and from the time of Nemanje it maintained strong links with Mount Athos. From the foundation of the Serbian archbishopric the power and influence of the Catholic Church began to decline and Orthodox monasteries and bishoprics were found up to the coast. When the Bogomils (see below) gained control in Bosnia, the Serbian state had only limited contact with the Catholics, Hungary in the north and the Angevins in Drac, Naples and Central Albania. However, when the Catholics were in a small minority in Serbia, the rulers were able to maintain friendly relations with the Papacy and take advantage of the position between East and West. One result was that Stephen First Crowned was able to obtain a crown from the Pope despite the opposition of the King of Hungary. On the other hand Stephen obtained a Serbian archbishopric from the Greeks. Another example of the willingness of the Serbian rulers to maintain contacts with the West was the alliance between Dushan and Charles of Valois; Dushan, anathemised by the Patriarch of Constantinople on the occasion of the creation of the Serbian Patriarchate, expressed his readiness to recognise the supremacy of the Pope.

Serbian kings always defended the Archbishop of Bar, especially when Dubrovnik tried to extend its rights over Bar territories. Dubrovnik complained in Rome that Urosh rejected Papal jurisdiction in his state and that his brother Vladislav had 'uttered words against the Pope and Cardinals'. In correspondence with the Pope, however, the newly appointed Archbishop of Bar described Dushan as 'our dear son in Christ the illustrious King of Serbia'. Relations with the West tended to be strengthened when the kings chose Western brides.

Relations between Serbia and the Papacy only became complicated when the Papacy was transferred to Avignon, virtually transforming the Pope into a French puppet; this was particularly the case when hostilities broke out between Serbia and the French Angevins now ruling in Hungary and Naples, especially during the reigns of Urosh II (1308) and Dushan from 1346. The Pope was unable to take advantage of the rift between Dushan and the Patriarch of Constantinople following the creation of the Serbian Patriarchate. Indeed the situation of the Catholics in the lands ruled by Dushan deteriorated. The Code laid down that 'concerning the Latin heresy any Christians who have turned to unleavened bread let him return to Christianity' and 'the Great Church shall appoint protopops to bring back Christians from the Latin heresy'. 'If a Latin priest converts a Christian let him be punished according to the laws of the Holy Fathers.' Latin priests were to be under the control of the Serbian monasteries. While Catholics might be permitted to practice their faith any attempt at proselyitism would be severely punished.

The Archbishop of Bar was appointed either by the Pope directly or by a Council of the Church of St. George. One such was William Adams, a Dominican from southern France and a bitter enemy of the 'schismatic' Greeks and Serbians, who spent much of his time away from Bar in France. The archbishops on the whole were chosen from the patrician families of

Bar. The bishops were divided into two groups: those who occupied the towns and fortresses lying close to one another on or near the coast, and those of the interior whose territories were scattered. From about 1200 these latter ceased to exist. The position of the bishops was made more difficult by internal quarrels; on one occasion citizens refused to accept the nomination of a particular bishop. One Dominican was accused of having taken part in a murder and was eventually forced to take refuge in Hungary when the Pope heard of it. For some of the poorer bishoprics it was difficult to find candidates. The Bishop of Skadar complained in 1349 that he lacked the means to live – though he was probably exaggerating – because his possessions were being seized. The Bishop of Balets complained that 'schismatics' from 'regnum Rassie' were reducing the income of his church. There were many Benedictine monasteries but there were frequent complaints of insufficient numbers of monks and the abbots appointed priests who had only lived two or three days in the monasteries. The abbots on the whole were chosen from the patrician families of Dubrovnik.

The bishopric of Kotor, lying between the mutually hostile archbishoprics of Dubrovnik and Bar, was subordinate from the 11th century to Bari in Italy, but remained nevertheless under the government of Serbia despite the opposition of some of the clergy. Kotor, thanks to the Serbian rulers, greatly expanded in the course of the 13th century. It included all the scattered Latin parishes and opatia in the Serbian state beyond the boundaries of the archbishopric of Bar, as well as the Latin churches and monasteries formerly under the jurisdiction of the Catholic Bishop of Trebinje and Hum lying within the state of Serbia. The bishopric of Budva, formerly under the jurisdiction of the Archbishop of Bar, was now joined to Kotor. But in the later 14th century the ability of the Serbian rulers to offer protection became weaker, and there were complaints from Kotor of the seizure of their possessions. In 1344 the Pope tried to obtain for Kotor the city of Budva with the monastery of St. Maria of Budva, and the much smaller monasteries and churches in the vicinity of the city of Trebinje and in Serbia itself.

While the relations between Serbia and Bar were friendly those with Dubrovnik were strained. The Latin bishopric of Trebinje, under the control first of Bar then Dubrovnik from 1200, was probably a victim of the struggle between Dubrovnik and the Serbian kings in the 13th century. In the 14th century the Bishop of Trebinje received two small Benedictine monasteries. Serbian Church properties beyond the frontiers of Dubrovnik were at first subordinate to the Catholic Bishop of Kotor, but were later moved from his jurisdiction. The Bishop of Kotor in 1346 attempted to obtain for himself the island of Molunat and the Benedictine monasteries near Trebinje. In one of the few references to women we find Dushan making a grant to a 'monasterium pulcellorum' of 100 perpers.

The attitude of the Serbian rulers, including Dushan, to the Catholic Church was ambiguous. On the one hand there is no evidence that any of them seriously contemplated conversion to Catholicism; on the other hand they were ready to use any means to gain Catholic support for political purposes. In view of the rivalry between the bishops and archbishops of the Catholic Church the kings could acquire a reputation for liberality and piety without any strengthening of the Catholic Church in their own lands. The Code is more indicative of Dushan's real attitude to the 'Latin heresy'.

One heresy which the Churches of the East and West were united in opposing was Bogomilism, which in the reign of Dushan had become virtually the national Church of Bosnia where it was known as the Pataren faith. Bogomilism was a dualist heresy originating in the Middle East whence it extended its influence to the eastern provinces of the Byzantine Empire, being particularly strong in Macedonia. Though it suffered a decline in Bulgaria as a result of the collapse of Samuel's empire, it revived in the 13th century following the establishment of the second Bulgarian Empire. By the 14th century however, it was once more in decline. It is probable that the sect entered Serbia as a result of links with Macedonia. Nevertheless Bogomilism failed to take root in Serbia, partly because of ruthless persecution, and partly because of the peculiar position of the Church in Serbia. These measures seem to have been effective for we hear no mention of the heresy until the reign of Dushan. Serbia was never as completely subordinate to Byzantium as was Bulgaria after the collapse of Samuel's empire; hence the hostility to things Greek was never so strong as in Bulgaria – though the sect was by no means 'nationalist' as we understand the term nor, as some modern Bulgarian historians claim, can it be seen as a popular revolt against Greek influence nor as an anti-feudal movement. In Serbia the Church was more national. 'By firmly establishing the Serbian Church on popular and national lines, St. Sava dealt the greatest possible blow to Bogomilism by depriving it of one of the most potent weapons of proselytism, the reaction against an excessive Byzantine influence on Church and State.' Furthermore the fact that Sava, the first Archbishop of Serbia, was the son of Nemanje, the fact that the latter and his son Stephen became monks established a link between the royal line and the Church which was lacking in Bulgaria. Clearly, however, Bogomilism was not completely dead in Serbia, if only because Dushan found it necessary in his Code to state that 'if any heretic be found living among Christians let him be branded in the face and driven forth' and while the word heretic can be applied to Catholics, the punishment meted out to these particular heretics makes it clear that it refers to Bogomils, since the punishment for proselyting Catholics as we know was much less severe. Bogomilism, lacking strong external support, could be dealt with ruthlessly; Catholicism, linked with the West, had to be treated more mildly.

From the time of the Nemanje, kings bore the title 'King of the Serbians' or 'King of the Serbian lands' or 'King of Serbian lands and the Pomori (Littoral)' that is, two groups of territories: Serbia proper (Ras) in the interior and the smaller principalities on the coast, the former being regarded as more important. The maritime territories included what the Byzantines called Dalmatia, comprising Duclea, Trebinje, Hum (the later Hercegovina) with the cities of Kotor, Bar and Skadar. Duclea (then later Zeta) was granted by Nemanje to his son Vukan on the same principle as in England with the Prince of Wales, and the widows of the Kings often retired there on the death of their husbands.

The smaller territorial units from which the State was ultimately to be were known as Zupas; these often comprised little more than a river valley and were sometimes divided into two parts, upper and lower in accordance with the course of the river from which they took their name in the majority of cases, e.g. Ras. The Zupas as important personages first appeared in the 12th century; with the growth of central power their importance diminished. The conquest of Greek territory, where no-one of comparable importance to the Zupans existed influenced the policy of the Serbian kings; these conquered territories were transformed into Zupas or 'oblast'. The Councils of the Zupas were in general only meetings for the purpose of registering royal decrees. Special duties were imposed on the governors of the frontier provinces, the 'kraj'. The Code of Dushan states that 'if any foreign armies come and ravish the lands of the Emperor and again return through these lands, these frontier lords shall pay all through whose territories they pass'. Frontiers were, of course, constantly changing. In the drive to the south the northern frontier tended to be neglected. A large part of the Adriatic coast was under Serbian control but decreased as a result of the expansion of Bosnia towards the coast. Serbian control extended from the mouth of the Drina to the northern bank of the Neretva estuary. Urosh called himself ruler 'a mare usque ad Danubii magni'. Dubrovnik alone maintained its independence. Dushan and Urosh IV proclaimed their right to the island of Mlet lying to the north-west of Dubrovnik. The north-west was the weakest of the frontiers because control of Hum was always uncertain and was finally lost to Serbia in the course of the Bosnian advance to the coast.

On the northern frontier the main threat came from the Hungarians and constant fighting occurred on the Sava and the Danube. Hungarian Bans ruled in the Banat of Machva which took its name from the city, but the most important city was Belgrade, strategically placed on the confluence of the Sava and the Danube. This territory was granted to Dragutin in 1286 as a vassal to the King of Hungary on the occasion of his marriage to the King's daughter. The Serbian kings were never able to gain permanent possession of Belgrade which remained in Hungarian hands until its capture by the Turks. In the south the frontiers with the Empire were much more elastic; Prizren fell to Serbia in the reign of Alexis III. The extension of the Serbian frontier began with the fall of Skopje in 1190; in the reign of Dushan the Serbian state included almost two thirds of the Balkan Peninsula.

The rulers, first as Great Zupans, later as Kings and finally as Emperors, were supreme war leaders, administrators, law givers and judges, and the greatest landowners in the State. Subjects owed him personal service and were obliged to accompany him on his journeys, provide him with food, etc. From the 12th century the succession was finally linked with the family of Nemanje. In the order of succession there was fusion of the simple theory of primogeniture and the Byzantine custom of joint rule. Struggles over the succession were frequent between brothers, fathers and sons. When, as sometimes happened, two brothers were jointly crowned as Kings, this was never satisfactory, one brother eventually establishing his predominance, for instance in the case of Dragutin and Milutin. The practice of crowning the heir as the young King (mladi kral) was not without its dangers, since there was a temptation to speed the process of inheritance by forcing the King into abdication or having him killed as in the case of Dushan with his father Stephen Decanski. Younger sons might be granted their own territories as happened in the case of Nemanje's brother Miroslav who was given Hum, and Nemanje's son Vukan who obtained Duclea. No attempt was made to establish independent principalities; in practice these areas became Zupas and the rulers bore the title of Zupans. The titles of the rulers changed; from the earliest period roughly from the eighth century to the 10th century they were called *archon* or *Dux* by the Byzantine emperors. With the ascendancy of Primorje the rulers proclaimed themselves as Kings 'Sclavorum rex' but this title disappeared completely after 1180, the last holder of the title being Vukan. The rulers of the eastern provinces, the true Serbian lands, the most important of which was Ras, were known as the Great Zupans, until Nemanje's son Stephen obtained a crown from the Pope in 1217. In accordance with Western custom the King was 'dominus rex' and owed his position to God by whose will he alone ruled.

Following the Byzantine example he had a whole string of honours, all of them religious: favoured of God, beloved of Christ and consequently invincible, 'rex invictissimus'. The term *autocrat*, the Byzantine form of the Roman Imperator, was included in the royal title of Stephen First Crowned,

King and autocrat (kral i samodrz'ts). Again following the example of the Byzantine emperors, the kings did not describe themselves in the first person singular nor as in the West by the royal plural, but as my majesty (kraljrvsto mi). On his death the King was automatically sanctified. The lands included in the royal title frequently changed; the presence of a territorial name in the title did not necessarily mean that the King actually ruled it – it could be regarded as a symbol of aspiration rather than a sign of achievement. Urosh called himself King of Croatia despite the fact that the country had never been conquered, and in fact recognised the King of Hungary as ruler. Similarly Albania often appeared in the title of Dushan and his half brother Simeon. Bulgaria appeared in the title of Urosh II in 1319 and not again till 1345 in Dushan's title. Finally on the strength of his conquest of some Byzantine territories Dushan styled himself Emperor of the 'Romans'.

Those who represented the King in the provinces were at once administrators, judges and commanders of the local forces, but did not control finances. In the time of Nemanje the word 'knez', generally translated as prince, referred to members of the ruling house. Later governors were called 'Vladats' (rulers) or 'Vladushti'. Changes developed in the administration of the Zupa; the old title of Zupan survived to the reign of Dushan, but in the Code the Zupa is only a territorial region and the Zupan was not recognised as the chief 'stareshina' of the region. While the Zupan system survived in Bosnia, in Serbia the administration changed; in place of the local landowner class the administrator was chosen by the King. The term for this position came from Byzantium; the word *kefali* appears as the name for commanders especially in the border towns such as Skopje and Skadar. Under Dushan this was replaced by the word namesnik or regent. Dushan's Code distinguishes two kinds of Zupas: those administered by kefali and those by 'vlastelin' in their own Zupas. As a result of Dushan's reforms juridical and administrative functions were separated. One duty of the kefali was to provide protection for travellers and to compensate for losses suffered. The word 'knez' varied in importance in the course of the 13th and 14th century. It was borne at one and the same time by members of the royal family and the administrators of towns and trading centres as well as leaders of the shepherds and villages. Under Dragutin and Urosh II the princes stood above the 'sebast' but the position seems to have been reversed under Dushan. The importance of the title can be seen from the fact that it was borne by the powerful Voislav and Lazar. Subordinate to the Zupan was the 'satnik' or captain. In 1186 the satnik represented Nemanje in the city of Kotor. Taxes were collected by the 'kazn'ts', a word which was translated in Dubrovnik as 'camerarius', possibly according to Jirecek of foreign perhaps Persian origin. Taxes were collected in the reign of Urosh II by an official known as the 'prator'; under Dushan he bore the title of 'globar'. Prior to the 11th century nothing is known of the courtly titles in Serbia, Duclea or Ras. The office of Ban, representative or regent of the ruler, appears in Croatia but never in Serbia; even for the 14th century our knowledge of courtly titles is very fragmented.

Serbian kings were not absolute rulers; their powers were limited by advisers and the National Council or Skupshtina. The Council of State in Serbia as well as in Bosnia and Croatia was the Sabor; other terms were 'okup, skup, shod' the latter most often appearing in Church texts suggesting, perhaps that it was confined to Councils dealing exclusively with Church affairs. Councils were of two kinds; those of the individual Zupas and those of the whole realm. The National Council had the task of filling a vacancy to the throne. The work of the Council of the Zupa was limited to the discussion of local affairs. Only freemen were eligible to take part in a coronation ceremony; later this privilege was confined to nobles. Under the Nemanje dynasty the old National Council corresponded to similar Councils in Hungary, Bulgaria and Bosnia, whereas in Byzantium, from which the Slav peoples of the Balkans borrowed so much, such Councils did not exist. The old title of 'protovastor' survived under Dushan. Apart from the Zupans of the separate Zupas, at court there was the Great Zupan; it is not known whether this title was reserved for members of the royal house; it was borne by one Dragish in the reign of Urosh II, and by Altimar in the reign of Dushan. One of the most important titles was that of commander of the army, the 'voivod', an office which might be held by more than one man as happened under Decanski and Dushan. Another title was that of 'sluga', literally servant, which may be compared with the Byzantine 'megas domesticos'. In addition a number of purely Byzantine titles existed, but these were only granted to the King's representatives in the captured Byzantine provinces in the south, never in the old Serbian territories. Examples of these were despot, sebastocrats and caesar; Urosh IV and Simeon the half brother of Dushan were granted the title of Despot and Simeon was appointed Despot of Epirus.

In the royal chancellory the main character was the 'logophet' responsible for correspondence; financial matters were dealt with by the protovastar; for each charter he received the sum of 30 perpers. Correspondence with the Dalmatian towns was conducted in Serbian and was dated after the Greek fashion. Charters were written in Greek when they dealt with the Byzantine emperors, the Despot of Epirus, the Archbishop of Ohrid, and when they granted privileges to Greek monasteries. Correspondence with the West was conducted in Latin with the help of the Dalmatians; one example was a letter to the titular Latin Emperor Charles of Valois in 1307. Under Dushan, Latin correspondence was entrusted to the Chancellor (komornik) or to the protovastar. On occasion the correspondence was conducted in two languages, Serbian and Latin as for example when the remuneration of Ston was granted to Dubrovnik. Relations with foreign states were conducted through ambassadors chosen from the leading men in the State; in negotiations with the West, men were chosen who understood Latin. Thus citizens of Kotor were selected to negotiate with Dubrovnik or Venice. In 1345 Dushan sent three ambassadors to the Pope in Avignon; a judge of the court, a Serbian kefali and a citizen of Kotor. Ambassadors might be chosen from the clergy; Sava made frequent journeys in the interests of his father Nemanje and his brother Stephen. Other examples were the Catholic Archbishop of Bar, sent to Naples by Urosh II and the Serbian bishop Danilo who went to Bulgaria and Constantinople.

The period which began with the Nemanje witnessed a transformation of a free peasantry and the development of a feudal order. The main evidence for this is to be found in the growth and development of monastic possessions. With the establishment of the autocephalous Church, new archbishoprics were created and granted large amounts of land not only from the King but from many of the great nobles. The Church, therefore, became one of the most powerful landowners in the State, controlling entire Zupas.

At the same time the nobles whose power and importance were steadily growing also increased their lands; apart from inheritance or lands seized by force, in which the peasants were transformed into serfs, nobles constantly received new lands as rewards for services rendered to the King. The greater part of the land undoubtedly belonged to the nobility. Such lands as were not in the possession of the nobles were directly owned by the King. He had his own family lands corresponding to the 'bashtina' or inherited lands of the nobles, where the peasants lived under conditions similar to those on noble lands. By the middle of the 14th century feudalism had been firmly established in Serbia; free peasants had virtually disappeared. The peasant 'kmet, sebar, rob' must have a master, king, nobles or the Church. One result of this was to tie the peasant to the village. Dushan's Code refers to this and the prohibitions against peasants living in the towns. The penalties for attempting to escape were ruthless, nevertheless do not seem to have been entirely effective in preventing peasants from moving from one land to another, a process which the feudal landowners sometimes helped. If the landowner did not claim his peasant within three years he forfeited his rights. These restrictions, however, did not apply to the Church.

The peasantry in Serbia was not a uniform class, being designated in law under different names: 'parik' or settler, people of the land 'zemalski ljudi'. The 'sebir' were peasants who were free economically and legally; the 'meropsi' were dependent peasants, often called simply 'ljudi'. There were three kinds of ljudi: ljudi kraljevstva, the people of the King, ljudi vlasteljci, people of the nobles, and ljudi crkovni, people of the Church. While ultimate ownership of the land lay with the King, nobles or the Church, the meropsi had ownership of the land he occupied in the sense that he could alienate it on condition that his successor fulfilled the duties linked with possession. He could not be prevented from doing so, his right was guaranteed by law. The meropsi enjoyed three rights; ownership, use and disposal, but there is some argument regarding the character of these rights and it has been suggested that he simply enjoyed the right of use. His duties towards his superior were of two kinds; the work rent involving labour on the lord's domain, and the natural rent under which he was normally obliged to pay a tenth of his produce. These burdens often forced the meropsi to flee; the lord lost the labour on which his existence depended and every effort was made to prevent such flights. They were illegal, though as we have seen, the three year limit might help anyone who managed to avoid capture for that period. At the same time there is evidence of movement from one lord to another; Church lands in particular were more attractive.

The legal status of the meropsi was probably better than that of the Western European serf. He had the right to leave the land subject to the permission of his lord, which admittedly was not likely to be easily obtained, and under the same conditions he could alienate his property, and finally he could call on the law to protect him even against his lord. Bearing in mind that the government was in the hands of, and defended the interests of the feudal class, such legal safeguards might not be very effective, nevertheless the fact that they existed is a recognition that in the eyes of the King the peasants did have rights. But while he enjoyed personal liberty, economically and politically he was subject to his lord.

The Vlach was the name given not only to an ethnic group distinct from the Serbians, but was applied generally to those engaged in stock breeding, and thus to a nomadic life. Special regulations existed to prevent damage to the village fields from the threat of pasture, and to regulate the relations between groups of herdsmen. Like the meropsi the Vlachs were dependent on their feudal lord for whom they supplied stock; this meant they were half settlers. Similarly they were burdened with feudal duties; they paid a pasture duty for their stock and provided work or other personal services for the Church, e.g. accompanying the monastic personnel on journeys. In reality the Vlachs and meropsi differed only in being engaged in different forms of agriculture. While 'racism' was not a feature of medieval Serbian life, marriage between Serbians and Vlachs appears to have been forbidden; when it happened the Vlach would become a meropsi.

At the bottom of the scale were the 'otroci' the serfs. Their legal position was not clear; some historians consider that slavery in the classical sense did not exist in medieval Serbia. This is merely a matter of definition; the otroci were under the control of their lord who could alienate them along with the land. In this sense they were like the Russian serf. Unlike the classical slave they were not completely without legal rights though whether and to what extent they benefited from this is an open question.

As in Western Europe town dwellers enjoyed more freedom than the peasants. This was particularly the case with foreigners like the 'Saxons', German miners who worked the mines and had the right to clear the forests. The coastal towns of the Adriatic were organised in a manner similar to neighbouring towns in Dalmatia, and were guaranteed their liberty to encourage trade.

The internal organisation of government changed with changes in political power. If we except the period of Dushan's reign there was a constant struggle between centralism and particularism. The three organs of power were the ruler, the National Council and the regional organs of government. The ruler expressed the political unity of all parts of the State; economically and politically he was supreme. The State was his patrimony from which he enjoyed all the benefits. Politically he was supreme because all power devolved from him. Under Dushan, Serbia was an absolute hereditary monarchy; but this absolute power had only been won as a result of a long internal struggle. Nemanje had been only Great Zupan, first among equals; his son had obtained a crown and recognition as independent ruler of Serbia. The crowning of Stephen was accompanied by the establishment of a Serbian archbishopric; Dushan's coronation as Emperor was followed by the establishment of the Serbian Patriarchate.

The Councils go back to the time of Nemanje; one such was called to discuss the problem of Bogomilism, which was seen as a political as well as a religious problem, a second on the occasion of Nemanje's abdication in favour of his son Stephen. They met frequently during the reign of Dushan. Membership of the Council was confined to nobles and clergy, and decided such important questions as changes of rulers, the appointment of leaders of the Church, the granting of lands to churches and monasteries, questions of privileges, legislation and questions of war and peace. It is not clear to what extent the Council limited the power of the ruler; all that can be assumed is that under a weak ruler the Council would enjoy more power than when the ruler was strong. Under Dushan it was largely an advisory body.

The Vlastela or nobles were not a compact class; the majority of these were known as 'vlastelicici' or small landowners possessing only one village or small property. Above them stood the great landowners, nobles in the true sense of the word, who were again divided into two groups: the 'velmoze' with wide scattered territories, and the smaller vlastela who occupied a position somewhere between the velmoze and the vlastelicici. All enjoyed equal rights but their power naturally depended on which group they belonged to. Grants of land could raise the status of the small landowners. The Code recognised some differences which did not encroach on the rights of the class as such; the great landowners were called in to judge in certain legal matters, whereas the small landowners sent only their seal. The latter were subject to punishment similar to those imposed on peasants.

The basis of the power of the great landowners was the right of inheritance, guaranteed by law; only in cases of treason could a noble be deprived of his land. In addition, land could be granted by the King in return for services; this was the *pronia,* copied from the system first introduced into Byzantium under which the proniar was liable either for military service or for supplying soldiers in proportion to the amount of land he held. Lands held under such conditions were not hereditary; heirs could be granted the land provided they were prepared to carry out the duties linked with its possession. Proniar attempted sometimes with success to transform the pronia into hereditary possessions. In addition to lands the ruler might make grants of Zupas or whole provinces from which the vlastela obtained part of the products which belonged to the King.

The Church was an important factor in feudal Serbia, its power and influence increased by the numerous grants of land made by rulers as a counterweight in the struggles with the nobles. Church lands, unlike those granted to nobles, belonged not to particular churches or monasteries but were considered as the property of the whole Church. Various members of the Church could, in exceptional circumstances, have their personal estates; for instance the Metropolitan Jacob of Serres personally obtained the monastery of St. Nicolas. The clergy enjoyed a privileged position in the State, being subject to Church law and trial by the Church courts. The leading clergy belonged to the landowning class while the lower clergy did not differ greatly from the peasantry. The leaders of the Church were the bishops and abbots of the great monasteries; they administered the Church and its properties; they represented the Church at the National Councils and exercised great influence on the ruler. Under them were the monks and the priests. Monks lived in monasteries where, apart from their religious duties, they exploited the monastical lands and were distinct from the laity. Isolated from their families, they were forced to enter a monastery away from the area in which they were born or where their family lived. They were exempt from taxation either by the Church or by the State. Leaders of the Church were drawn from the ranks of the monks because they alone could become abbots of the monasteries or bishops.

Priests by the nature of their duties were less isolated from the world. Burdened with a family and scattered through the land, their position in the feudal hierarchy was more dependent than that of the monks. They could be divided into two categories, depending on whether they had their free inheritance; those possessing no land obtained it from the lord on whose territory their parish lay. If this were not granted they could, subject to the intervention of the Bishop, leave their master. The duties and restrictions incumbent upon the priest put him in a position similar to that of the peasant, and like the latter, part of the produce of the land went to the Bishop. The dependent position of the priest was clearly confirmed in the Code; only those in possession of inherited lands were free. Those granted lands by their lord were not liable for work on the land, but the land they worked retained the burdens which fell on it. If a priest took more than the specified amount of land he had to work it according to the law like a peasant. Finally the sons of priests who did not follow their fathers into the priesthood entered the ranks of the peasantry.

Economic Development

In southern Serbia the old towns were of Greek or Roman origin. In the north towns developed as a result of trade or mining. Roman towns under Serbian rule continued to enjoy the wide measure of autonomy they possessed under the rule of Byzantium, having their own territorial limits, their own legal system, judges and administration chosen by them annually. Power was confined in the 14th century to the Great Council, a closed body of aristocrats. The ruler was represented by the 'knez' or prince who need not necessarily be a citizen of the city. In view of their commercial importance Serbian kings were careful to preserve the autonomy of the coastal cities of the Adriatic. The cities under the jurisdiction of the Archbishop of Bar were in a special position, consisting as they did of Romans, Albanians and Slavs, more rarely Greeks. Skadar because of its geographical position was from the time of the Romans and Illyrians the natural centre of the area. Ulcini was rich in wheat and oil and wine; first in importance, however, was Bar.

Trade in Serbia was boosted when Nemanje granted freedom of trade to the merchants of Dubrovnik. Serbian trading links were especially strong with Prizren and Pech which were under the protection of the Church. Trading relations between Prizren and Dubrovnik are frequently referred to while Pech also established relations with Venice. Mining was an important source of trade and Novo Brdo in particular had links stretching from Salonika and Bulgaria to the Adriatic coast. In the mountainous areas of the west the Vlachs traded in cattle in exchange for manufactured goods. The towns under the jurisdiction of the Archbishop Bar carried on a lively trade. Kotor, however, in the time of the Nemanje was by far the most important trading centre.

The importance which Serbian rulers attached to trade is confirmed by the privileges granted to foreign traders in Serbia. The colonies of such traders were subject to their own laws in internal questions. In the 13th and 14th centuries the Venetians maintained their consuls in Kotor and Ulcini; Dubrovnik maintained a consul in Serbia itself. A 'consul general' existed for the whole land with the power to decide questions involving disagreements between merchants. The consul was prohibited from engaging in trade himself and was obliged to accompany the King on his travels. Trading links were now stronger with the West than with the immediate neighbours of Serbia. There is no evidence of trade with Hungary or Bulgaria; trade between Serbia and Byzantium was more important and Greek merchants, perhaps from Salonika, visited the fairs in Skopje and Prizren. Drac, which for some time was in the hands of the Angevins of Naples, exported salt throughout the whole surrounding area; commercial links between Serbia and Drac were established through the mediation of Dubrovnik.

Among the 'Latin' cities Dubrovnik took pride of place – from 1205-1358 under the rule of Venice. The geographical position of Dubrovnik made it the most important trading centre in Dalmatia; the only Dalmatian city with free access to the open sea, and more protected by the mountains in the rear than Kotor or Split, it could only be attacked from the sea, and never formed part of Serbia even under Dushan, since Serbian naval power was never adequate to the purpose. The policy of Dubrovnik was to extend the borders to the mountains, thus establishing a natural defensible frontier to protect their vineyards. The attempts of Serbian rulers to limit the expansion of Dubrovnik proved fruitless. Frontier disputes often led to hostilities since the inhabitants of neighbouring areas, Trebinje and Hum, regarded the attempts of Dubrovnik to extend its frontiers as a threat to themselves. Stephen Radislav confirmed the vineyards in the Serbian lands of those citizens whose fathers and grandfathers had held them but forbade further expansion. When the war between Serbia and Dubrovnik ended in

1254 the citizens of Dubrovnik were allowed to retain the lands held at the time of the death of Stephen First Crowned; ownership of lands seized after that period would be decided by law. Nevertheless the border question remained unsolved. In 1349, in the charters dealing with commercial matters, the main subjects were customs duties and questions of administration. By an agreement of 1302 merchants domiciled in Serbia were exempt from the duty of building towns and military service and their horses and goods could not be requisitioned. If a merchant was robbed he had to be compensated by the inhabitants of the nearest village; should the villagers be unable or unwilling to pay, compensation would be paid by the King. Vineyards were subject to similar protection and in 1326 this protection was extended to ships.

The bulk of Dubrovnik's trade by land went to the fortified towns extending from the mouth of the Neretsa and Bosnia to southern Hungary, and in Serbia up to the valleys of the Morava and Sharplonin. In Bulgaria, where trade was largely in the hands of the Genoese, Dubrovnik merchants are mentioned only in Vidin. Macedonia seems to have been virtually closed to them, probably because trade there was in the hands of the Greeks. Among the Dalmatian cities the links between Serbia and Split and Trogir were comparatively weak. Zadar traded by sea with Kotor, Bar and Drac, and, through Dubrovnik, handled exports from Serbia.

Venice was the main power in the Adriatic, maintaining its security with a powerful navy. There are no records of direct trade between Venice and Serbia, communications being maintained mainly through Dubrovnik and Kotor. Nevertheless the importance of Slav-Venetian trade in the 14th century is confirmed by the existence of a special department in Venice, the 'fonticum Sclavorum'. The valuable trade in slaves from 'Sclavonia' to Venice was carried on through Dubrovnik, in consequence of which the merchants of the latter were freed from the payment of customs duties. Under the customs regulations of 1277 Venetians in Dubrovnik enjoyed great freedom. In Kotor relations with Venice were regulated by a series of agreements confirmed by the Serbian kings in 1335, 1345 and 1348. Nevertheless disputes often arose. When the Council of Kotor were unwilling for some reason to pay for salt the Venetians forbade further exports to the city, refused further credit and threatened to confiscate goods belonging to Kotor at present in Dubrovnik.

Direct Serbo-Venetian relations beyond the coastal cities, apart from political questions – particularly the attempt by Dushan to form an alliance with Venice against Byzantium – were concerned with the sale of arms. The Venetians were annoyed when after 1282 the Serbians began to imitate Venetian coinage. Conflict also arose over the plundering by servants of the Serbian coastal bishops of Venetian ships which had run aground. Through the intervention of Urosh II and his son, agreement was reached under which the Bishop of Zeta would pay 4,000 Venetian *soldi grossorum;* the cattle which the Bishop offered in lieu of payment were only valued at some 1,200 soldi, and when sold realised only 800 perpers. The ambassador sent to obtain the compensation complained of being cheated, and the Venetians were still complaining of it 10 years later. In 1271 a complaint was lodged to the 'rex Rascie' over alleged ill treatment of a Venetian citizen in Serbia, while in 1318 when an ambassador from Kotor was sent to Venice, the Doge refused to meet him because of the alleged failure to satisfy Venetian complaints over the devastation of the coastal areas. The situation deteriorated to such an extent that the Venetians in Dubrovnik and the latter merchants themselves were forbidden to trade 'in terras regum Radcie' and 'regina matris eorum (Queen Helen)'. In 1314 Venetians were forbidden to travel in Serbia and the ban on trade continued until 1326.

Foreign merchants in Serbia were of two kinds; the small traders who generally traded in villages and in the neighbourhood of their towns, and the second group consisting of the great merchants with considerable means and numerous escorts. The majority of these merchants belonged to trading companies containing members from various towns and areas. Citizens of Kotor for instance combined with those of Drac, Venice or Dubrovnik, citizens of Dubrovnik with Venetians, Serbians, Vlachs and Albanians.

Security of communications was greater in the Adriatic than in the Aegean which was infested with pirates, Italian, Greek, and from the 14th century Turks. Responsibility for clearing the seas devolved mainly on the Venetians, the chief naval power in the Adriatic, but in spite of all their efforts pirates continued to disturb the peace. They came mainly from Ormish in Croatia until it fell to the Venetians in 1281, but they also operated further afield in Sicily and Catalonia. Trade was carried on as a monopoly and strictly regulated and exports were ultimately subordinate to politics. From time to time the export of metal was prohibited. A certain Venetian, Danilo Dioci was unable to dispose of a quantity of lead which he had sold to a citizen of Kotor because all the lead was required for the roof of the monastery of Prizren. The City Councils of the coastal towns strictly controlled the sale of wine to protect their products and the import of wine into Dubrovnik was strictly forbidden. Similar action was taken by other areas in defence of their interests. Trade in foodstuffs in the area of Dalmatia was limited and restricted in a manner similar to the custom in Italy, where the trade in such things as wine, salt, and oil was a government monopoly; in Apuleia exports required the permission of the King of Naples. In Kotor the export of foodstuffs was prohibited by sea. In the negotiations between Dushan and Dubrovnik it was agreed that wine and wheat should be sold for the same value in Serbia as in Dubrovnik. Under normal circumstances the export of wheat was not restricted; the merchants of Dubrovnik were permitted 'to buy wheat in the lands and towns of my kingdom freely'. Anyone attempting to prevent trade would be fined the sum of 500 perpers.

Serbia at this period was essentially an exporter of primary products. These consisted in the first place of horses, livestock which were exported via Dubrovnik to southern Italy, lamb and buffalo skins, tallow, fat, wool and cheese. Fish was an important export in the coastal regions from Bohanje to Valona. From Serbia and Bosnia as well as Bulgaria, Greece and Albania came wax and honey in great quantities. Wood, especially for shipbuilding, came from the interior and was sold on the coast where it was shipped from Dalmatia by sea to Greece, Italy, Sicily and Malta. Agricultural products did not figure prominently in exports from the Balkans, exports of wheat coming mainly from Albania, the Pelepennese, the coast of Macedonia, Thrace and the Black Sea areas. Slaves, male and female, were exported for the most part from Bosnia; they were sold by the Ban and the families of the slaves themselves. The main markets were in Kotor and Dubrovnik, other markets being Venice, Apuleia and Sicily. Under a statute of 1273 the Prince of Dubrovnik received a special tax on slaves transported by sea, according to their size. Slavery was widespread in Italy. Apart from the Tatar areas and the Caucasus, slaves from Greece and the northern Balkan lands were found throughout Italy. The Christian conscience of those who purchased the slaves was less troubled where the slaves were adherents of the Bogomil heresy, which may explain the predominance of Bosnians among the slaves, since Bogomilism was firmly established in Bosnia, and large numbers of them were to be found in Dubrovnik and Kotor. The Code of Dushan prohibited the sale of Christians to unbelievers; otherwise there seems to have been no restrictions placed on the trade. South Slav traders, indeed, enjoyed special privileges from Dubrovnik, a clear indication of the advantages accruing to the city from this trade. Traders were exempt from payment of taxes on the import, export and sale of slaves; these were paid by the purchaser.

One sign of the increasing development of trade was the use of minted coinage from the 13th century. But traces are still to be found of the old pre-monetary system of barter where the main unit of value was the horse; we find an example of a merchant of Dubrovnik exchanging a horse for a quantity of fabric, and horses were exchanged for slaves. Barter was common in the mountainous areas inhabited by the Vlachs where the merchants of Dubrovnik exchanged salt for livestock. The horse remained an important unit of value even after the general use of money but more as a symbol. From a charter of 1220 we find that fines must be paid with horses or oxen. Dushan ordered the monastery of the Archangel near Prizren to grant a horse to the Patriarch when he visited the monastery, and to the

Metropolitan 12 perpers or a foal. The Vlachs were obliged to make an annual gift of a horse to Dushan, the value of which was estimated at from 12-13 perpers. The gift of a horse was symbolically important on the occasion of the accession of the ruler, the granting of honours or lands. Oxen for the payment of fines still appear in the charters of Milutin but in a later charter of the King we find that a fine must be paid in money. The general exception to this rule seems to have been the Vlachs who, if convicted of theft, had to pay fines in horses or oxen.

Bibliography

Adams (W.). Directorium ad passagium faciendum, *in* Recueil des Historiens des Croisades: Documents Armeniens II.

Baynes (N. H.) and Moss (HSt L. B.) Moss. Byzantium: An introduction to East Roman Civilisation. London, 1969.

Bogdanovich (D.). Stara Srpski Biografije (Early Serbian Biographies). Belgrade, 1975.

Cambridge Medieval History: vol. IV. London, 1967.

Culinovic (F.). Drzavnoprava Historija Jugoslavenskih Zemlja (Constitutional History of Yugoslavia). Zagreb, 1961.

Danilo (Archbishop). Zivoti Kraljeva i Arhiespiskopa Srpskih (Lives of the Serbian Kings and Archbishops). Ed. D. Dinicic. London, 1972.

Diehl (C.). L'Europe Orientale de 1081 a 1453. Paris, 1945.

Dinits (M.). Odnos izmedje Dragutina i Milutina (Relations between Dragutin and Milutin) *in* Zbornik Radova Vizantoloshki Institut III (Collection of the Works of the Byzantine Institute). Belgrade, 1955.

ibid. Srpske Zemlje u Srednjem Veku (Serbian Lands in the Middle Ages). Belgrade, 1978.

Dvornik (F.). Les Slaves: Histoire et Civilisation. Paris, 1968.

Florinskii (T.). Juznye Slavanje vo vtoroj cetverti XIV veka (The South Slavs in the second quarter of the 14th century). London, 1973.

Hilferding (A.). Istoriya Serbor i Bolgar (History of the Serbians and the Bulgarians). St. Petersburg, 1868.

Historija Naroda Jugoslavije I (History of the Yugoslav People). Zagreb, 1953.

Hungarian Academy of Science. History of Hungary. London, 1975.

Istorija Jugoslavije (History of Yugoslavia). Belgrade, 1973.

Istorija Makedonskog Naroda (History of the Macedonian People) I. Belgrade, 1970.

Jirecek (C.). Istorija Srba (History of Serbia). Belgrade, 1978. Translation of two works which originally appeared in German: Geschichte der Serben, and Staat und Gesellschaft in Mittelalterlichen Serbien, translated by Jovan Radonich.

Kreckiv (B.). O Ratu Dubrovnika i Srbije, 1327-28 (On the War between Dubrovnik and Serbia, 1327-28) *in* Zbornik Radova Vizantoloshkog Institut XI (Collection of the Works of the Byzantine Institute). Belgrade, 1968.

Mihaljchits (R.). Kraj Srpskog Tsarstva (End of the Serbian Empire). Belgrade, 1975.

Mijushkovich (J. K.). Beograd u Srednjem Veku (Belgrade in the Middle Ages). Belgrade, 1967.

Mirkovic (M.). Ekonomska Historija Jugoslavije (Economic History of Yugoslavia). Zagreb, 1968.

Nicol (D. M.). The Last Centuries of Byzantium. London, 1972.

Obolensky (D.). The Bogomils. London, 1972.

ibid. The Byzantine Commonwealth: Eastern Europe, 500-1453. London, 1971.

Ostrogorsky (G.). Istorija Vizantije (History of Byzantium). Belgrade, 1969.

ibid. Vizantija i Sloveni (Byzantium and the Slavs). Belgrade, 1970.

Pavlovich (D.) and Marinkovich (R.). Iz nasha knjivenost Feudalnog Doba (From our literature of the Feudal Period). Belgrade, 1975.

Popovich (D.). Srbi u Voivodina (The Serbians in Voivodina). Novi Sad, 1957.

Pukovich (M.). Jelena Zena Tsara Dushana (Helen, wife of the Emperor Dushan). Dusseldorf, 1975.

ibid. Srpski Patrijarci Srednjega Veka (Serbian Patriarchs of the Middle Ages). Windsor, Canada, 1958.

Soloviev (A.) and Moshin (V.). Grcke Povelje Srpskih Vladara (Greek Charters of the Serbian Rulers). Belgrade, 1936.

Soulis (G. C.). Tsar Stephen Dushan and Mount Athos, in Harvard Slavic Studies, II. 1954.

Uspenski (F. I.). Obrazovanye Vtorogo Bulgarskago Tsarstva (Formation of the Second Bulgarian Empire). Odessa, 1879.

Vasiliev (A. A.). History of the Byzantine Empire. Madison, 1964.

Zakonik. The Code of Stephen Dushan. Ed. by S. Novakovich. English translation by M. Burr in Slavonic and East European Review, 1950. London, 1950.

Index of Names

ADAMS, William, 17, 18, 24, 27, 118
Albrecht, claimant to Hungarian throne, 97, 101
Alexis Angelos, son of Emperor Isaac, 6, 8
Alexis Angelos, Byzantine Emperor, 8, 122
Andrew, younger brother of King of Hungary, 7, 10-11, 12
Andronicus I, Palaeologus, 3, 4
Andronicus II, Palaeologus, 22-23, 25-26, 31, 69, 116
Andronicus III, Palaeologus, 26-28, 32-33, 69, 73
Andronicus Cantacuzene, Domestos, 42
Anna, Byzantine Empress, 33, 37, 44, 64
Avakov, 37, 38
Asen, Tsar of Bulgaria, 3, 8, 12-13, 41, 50, 67-68, 70-71, 87

BAJAZID, son of Murad, 93-96, 100, 104-105
Baldwin, Latin Emperor, 9, 13, 15
Balsha Balshici, 86, 96
Balshici, family, 86-89, 90
Bela III, King of Hungary, 4-6
Bogden Caesar, 65, 67
Bogomils, Religious Sect, 71, 120, 133
Boniface, Count of Montferrat, 8-9
Boril, Tsar of Bulgaria, 11-12

CAESAR Vojihan, 88
Carlo Topija, 87

Casimir, King of Poland, 79
Chag, son of Nogaj, 20
Charles II, claimant to Hungarian throne, 21, 32
Charles IV, King of Bohemia, 72
Charles V, Holy Roman Emperor, 107
Charles, of Anjou, 15-17, 21-23
Charles Martel, son of Charles II, 21
Charles Robert, of Hungary, 25-28, 32, 72-75
Chomatonos, Patriarch, 11
Chrel, vassal of Dushan, 33-34
Clement IV, Pope, 74, 77
Constantin Asen, 116
Constantin, eldest son of Milutin, 27
Constantin Dejanovich, 93

DANILO, Bishop, 115, 125
Decanski, see under Stephen Urosh Decanski
Demetrius, son of Empress Irene, 23
Deijan Sebastocrat, 67
Dimitir, son of Vukashin, 100
Dragash, brothers, John and Constantin, 89-90, 92-93
Dragutin, see under Stephen Dragutin
Drman, Bulgarian Boyar, 20

ELENA, sister of Stephen Dushan, married Mladin of Croatia, 79
Elena, wife of Stephen Urosh IV, 79
Elizabeth, wife of Louis of Hungary, 76

Eudokia, wife of Stephen First Crowned, 6, 9

FABIAN, secretary to John Nenad, 112
Ferdinand of Habsburg, 106-107, 109, 113
Frederick Barbarossa, German Emperor, 3-6
Frederick, Emperor, 103-104

GEORGE Balshici, 86-88, 93
George Brankovich, 95-99, 101-102, 104-105
George Dozda, commander of Hungarian army, 105
George Terter, ruler of Bulgaria, 20-21
Gregoras Palamis, Archbishop of Salonika, 39, 47, 62, 68, 117
Gregory, Pope, 89

HELEN, wife of Stephen Dushan, 16, 45, 50, 67-68, 82-85, 88
Helen, wife of Urosh I, 20, 24
Henry, Latin Emperor, 9, 11
Hesycasts, religious sect, 117

IMRE, King of Hungary, 10
Innocent III, Pope, 8, 78-79
Irene, Byzantine Empress, 23
Irene Cantacuzene, 39, 70
Isaac Angelos, Byzantine Emperor, 3-6, 8
Istvan Bathory, 106-107
Ivan (Janko) Hunyadi, 97-98, 101-102
Ivan Talovats, 97
Ivanish Berislavich, 105
Ivanish Uleg, son of Mathias, 104

JACOB, son of Sultan Murad, 93
Jacob, Metropolitan of Serres, 128
John Asen Alexander, 41
John Cantacuzene, 31, 33-40, 53, 55-66, 68, 75, 81, 84, 114, 117
John Capistrini, Franciscan friar, 102

John Comnenos Asen, 83
John Dolich, 112
John Hoberdanits, 107, 112, 113
John Nenad, 106-107, 109-113
John Palaeologus, Byzantine Emperor, 33, 35, 38, 59, 62, 64, 68-69, 84
John Shishman, son of Alexander Asen, 87
John Skenderbeg, 104
John Stratismir, son of Alexander Asen, 87

KALLISTOS, Patriarch of Constantinople, 87
Kalojan, Tsar of Bulgaria, 8-10
Katerina, wife of Stephen Dragutin, 18, 21
Katsijaner, General, 109
Kudelin, Bulgarian Boyar, 20

LADISLAV (Louis), King of Hungary, 26, 55-56, 72-79, 84-87, 91-92, 104
Ladislav Chakiije, 110
Ladislav Jagellon, 102, 104-106
Laza Lazarovich, 94
Lazar Chrebljanovich, 89, 91-94, 123
Lazar Mrnjavchevich, Despot, 87, 89
Lazarovich, son of Stephen Lazar, 94-96
Louis IV, of Hungary, murder of, 21

MANFRED, King of Sicily, 15, 17
Manuel, brother of Theodore of Epirus, 13
Manuel II, Byzantine Emperor, 89
Manuel Cantacuzene, son of John Cantacuzene, 34, 37-38, 39
Manuel Liver, Voivod of Valera, Serres, Strum, 42
Maria, wife of Vuk Brankovich, 109
Maria, wife of Stephen Decanski, 27

Maria, wife of Frederick of Habsburg, 109, 111
Mario, brother of John, Despot of Srem, 105
Marko, son of Vukashin, 89-90, 93-95
Mathias Korvin, King of Hungary, 103-104
Matija Cantacuzene, sister of John Cantacuzene, 84
Michael Anodjelovich, 99
Michael Asen, son of Tsar Alexander of Bulgaria, 67, 69
Michael, Tsar of Bulgaria, 28
Michael of Epirus, 14-16
Michael Palaeologus, 15, 19
Militsa, wife of Stephen Lazar, 94
Milutin, see under Stephen Urosh Milutin
Miroslav, brother of Stephen Nemanje, 122
Mladin, Ban of Croatia, 53, 79
Mrnjavchevich, family, 86
Muhamed II, Sultan, 98
Muhamed Andjelov, Turkish leader, 99
Muhamed, brother of Sulemein, 95-96
Murad, Sultan, 87, 93, 96-98
Musa, brother of Sulemein, 95-96

NEMANJE, see under Stephen Nemanje
Nicephor, Despot of Epirus, 63
Nicephorus II, Orsen, 81-85
Nicholas V, Pope, 102
Nicodemus, Archbishop, 25
Nicola Altomanovich, 89-91, 93
Nogaj, Tartar ruler, 20-21

OLIVER, brother of Helen wife of Stephen Dushan, 34, 45, 52, 56, 67

PAUL Bakich, Despot, 108-109
Peter, King of Aragon, 17
Peter, Bishop, 79

Peter, of Courtney, 11
Peter, Tsar of Bulgaria, 3-5, 8
Peter Perenje, Voivod, 111-113
Philip, son of Baldwin II, 17
Philip, of Tarento, 22, 26-27
Preljub, Regent of Thessaly, 81-82, 85
Prilep, Despot, 57-58

RADICH Bozich, 108, 111
Radich Brankovich Rastislavich Rastislalic, 92-93
Radislav, son of Stephen First Crowned, 11-14, 20
Rastislalic, family, 84-85
Rastislav, son of Nemanje, see under Sava

SAMUEL, Tsar of Bulgaria, 1, 70, 120
Sava St., son of Stephen Nemanje, 6-7, 10, 12-13, 19, 114, 120, 130
Sava II, Archbishop of Serbia, 63-70
Shishman, ruler of Vidin, 20, 69, 71
Sigismund, King of Hungary, 92, 94, 96-97, 100-101
Simeon, Tsar of Bulgaria, 1, 3, 41, 48, 70
Simeon Palaeologus, 56, 81-83, 85, 124
Simonides, wife of Stephen Milutin, 21-24, 26-27
Sirgian, 31-32
Skenderbeg, 104
Smil (Smilep), 20-22
Stephen, Ban of Bosnia, 27, 75-76, 80
Stephen Dragutin, 15-21, 23-25, 73, 116, 122-123
Stephen Dushan, 2, 22, 29-33, 35-39, 43-58, 60-68, 70-73, 76-85, 114-119, 121-125, 127, 130, 133-134
Stephen Lazarovich, son of Lazae, 94-96, 100-101
Stephen Radoslav, 130
Stephen Urosh I, 13-16, 49, 115-116

Stephen Urosh II, Milutin, 15,
17-27, 50, 67, 115-116, 122, 125,
132-134
Stephen Urosh III, Decanski, 24-25,
27-30, 50, 67-68, 116, 122-131
Stephen Urosh IV, 41, 45, 76,
82-88, 121-124
Stephen Vukchich, 98
Stratsimir Balshici, 86
Strez, Bulgarian traitor, 11
Sulemein, Sultan, 61, 95, 106

TAMURLANE, 95
Tatars, 71, 79
Theodora, wife of Stephen
Decanski, 21, 27
Theodora, wife of Uglesh
Mrnjavchevich, 67
Theodore, Despot of Epirus, 10,
12-13
Theodore Lascaris, 15
Theodore, son of Empress Irene, 23
Trvtko, claimant to Serbian throne,
91-94
Tsrnojevich, family, 97

UGLESH, brother of Vukashin, 45,
67, 86, 88-89, 91, 93
Ulrich Celli, Hungarian magnate,
101

VALENTIN Terek, 108, 110, 112
Villhardin, Prince of Achaea, 15
Vlachs, 126, 133-134
Vladislav, son of Stephen Dragutin,
18, 24-25, 27
Vladislav, son of Stephen First
Crowned, 13-14
Vladislav III, King of Hungary, 97
Vlaska Vlach, Prince, 79
Vlastela (Nobles), 128
Voisil and Montenegro, 20
Vojihinovich Voislav, 86, 90
Vuk Brankovich, Despot of Serbia,
90-95, 98-99, 103-104
Vuk Lazarovich, son of Stephen
Lazar, 95
Vuk, son of Stephen Nemanje, 7, 9,
121-122
Vukashin, Despot, 45, 86-88, 91, 93

WILLIAM II, King of Sicily, 3

ZAKONIK (Code) of Stephen
Dushan, 57, 115, 118, 121, 125,
128, 133
Zarko, Serbian noble, 85
Zealots Radical Party in Salonika,
31, 38, 57, 60

Index of Places

ADRIANOPLE, 13-14, 65, 69-70
Akernan, 76
Albania, 5, 7, 12, 15-16, 26, 32-33, 40, 51, 54, 61, 69, 76, 87, 89, 97, 101, 118, 123, 133
Angora, 95, 100
Arkan, 56
Athos, Mount, 42-44, 46, 116-117
Avlon, 33

BANAT, Serbian settlement, 100, 103
Bar, 5, 15, 86, 117-119, 121, 125, 129-131
Belgrade, 13, 17, 25-26, 73, 92, 95-98, 100-102, 105-106, 122
Berat, 10, 83, 90
Bosnia, 2, 3, 6-7, 17, 24, 26, 27, 29, 47, 50, 53, 55, 59-60, 61-62, 72-76, 91, 97-99, 104-105, 117, 120, 121, 123-124, 131, 133
Brach, 2, 50
Branichev, 10, 20, 85, 97, 103
Buda, Council of (1527), 97, 104, 106-107
Buda, Capture of, 108, 112-113
Budva, 86, 119

CHALCIDIC, 65-66
Christopol, 35, 38-39, 41, 84
Constantinople, Capture of (1453), 98
Croatia, 53-54, 94, 104, 123-124

DEBAR, 12, 20
Decani Monastery, 28, 116
Diampol, 28

Dimitok, 65, 70
Drac, 11, 13-15, 32, 87, 118, 130-132
Drachevic, 90-91
Dram, 20, 84
Dubrovnik, relations with Serbia, 13-16, 19, 27, 28-30, 40, 45, 47-50, 60, 71, 83, 85-86, 96-98, 114, 117-118, 119, 123, 125
Dubrovnik, trade with Serbia, 130, 132-133
Duclea, see under Zeta

EDESSA, 34-35, 62
Epirus, 9-15, 26, 32-35, 55, 57, 60, 63, 75-76, 82-84, 124
Erdelj, battle of (1437), 97, 112
Etoli, despotate, 56, 76

GORIANA, battle of, 109
Golubats, 92, 96, 100-101

HILANDER, 7, 25, 46, 87, 115-117
Hum, 2, 7, 13, 16, 27, 40, 74-76, 81, 90, 115-116, 119, 121-122, 130
Hvar, 2, 49-50

KANIN, 33, 56
Kephalin, 80
Kicevo, 20, 22
Klios, 79-80
Knin, 53
Kolubar, 25
Konavlje, 90-91
Korcula, 2
Kosovo, 5, 92-93

Kosovo, battle of (1389), 95, 98, 102, 116
Kossnits, Council of (1414), 100
Kostur, 31, 82, 88
Kotor, 2, 5, 29, 51, 53, 54, 56, 86, 90-91, 119, 121, 123, 125, 130-133
Krc, Island of, 48

LESBOS, 32
Ljesh, 96

MACHVA, 15-18, 73, 94-96, 100-101, 122
Maritsa, battle of, 65-66, 89
Mesembria, 2, 28
Mlet, Island of, 2, 28, 121
Mohacs, battle of, 106, 108, 110-111
Mostar, 13

NAPLES, 72, 74, 118
Nicaea, 10-11, 14-15, 114
Nicopolje, battle of, 94
Nin, 50
Nish, 4, 10-11, 93, 96
Novo Brdo, 92, 96-99, 102, 130

OHRID, 10-14, 28, 31-32, 41, 43-44, 46, 88, 114-115, 117, 124
Osor, Island of, 48
Ovecpol, granted to Milutin, 22

PECH, Archbishopric of, 114, 130
Philipol, 71
Phocus, 32
Plevna, 15
Plochnik, battle of (1386), 93
Podgora, 2
Polog, 22
Porec, 20
Prilep, 14, 31-32, 87-88
Pristrin, 34
Prizren, 5, 10, 43, 86-90, 93, 115-116, 122, 130, 132-133

RAB, Island of, 48
Ras, 2-3, 6-7, 11, 18, 85, 93, 101, 115-116, 121, 124

Rhodop, 71
Ril, Monastery of, 34
Rovina, battle of (1325), 94
Rudnik, 23, 92

SALONIKA, 3, 9, 12-13, 23, 31-40, 56-57, 60-65, 73, 75, 117, 130
Sarajevo, 103, 116
Segedon, 113
Serres, 33-36, 38-41, 42-43, 45, 47, 53, 83-85, 87-88, 116, 128
Shapats, 26, 103
Shebenik, 50
Skadar, 5, 19, 27, 83, 86, 96, 119, 121, 123, 129
Skopje, 5, 10, 12, 13, 19, 22, 39, 41, 43, 61-62, 87-90, 93-94, 96-97, 117, 122-123, 130
Skradan, 48, 79-80
Smederov, 97-100, 102-103, 105, 108
Split, 14, 48, 50, 130-131
Srebnits, 96, 103
Srem, 13, 23, 103-106, 107, 108-110
Stefiano, battle of, 39, 63
Ston, 28, 74, 86, 90-91, 115-116, 125
Strumnits, 31, 34, 39
Studenica Monastery, 7, 115
Subotnits, expulsion of Turks from, 110

TATI, agreement of (1427), 96, 100-101
Temishvar, 103
Thessaly, 13, 32-34, 36, 55, 57, 61-63, 75-76, 82-84
Timok, 96
Toplic, 7, 93, 115-116
Trebinje, 2, 7, 13, 74, 86, 90-91, 119, 121, 130
Tripolje, battle of, 95
Trnovo, 4, 15, 41, 43-44, 94
Trnovo, Council of (1211), 71

ULCINJ, 92, 129, 130

VALONA, 83, 90
Varna, battle of (1444), 102
Vatoped Monastery, 6, 46
Velbuzd, battle of, 28, 30-31, 66, 69
Veles, 14
Venice, Relations with Dushan,
　47-57, 58-61, 63-64, 66, 71, 74-75,
　77-79, 83, 85, 90-91, 96-98, 105,
　125, 130, 131-133
Verri, 36-39, 61-62
Vidin, 15, 20, 87, 131

Vienna, 107-109, 112
Vlach, 33, 55, 57, 78, 126-127

ZADAR, 7-8, 30, 48-49, 52-53,
　54-55, 56, 131
Zeta, 2, 5, 7, 21, 24, 25, 27, 40, 83,
　85-86, 96-98, 101, 115-116, 121,
　132
Zich, 12, 20, 114-115
Zihn, 38-39